Celebrity Court Cases:
The Psychology of Why We Watch

Raqota Berger

Published by Armbar
P.O. Box 1041
Los Angeles, Ca.
91376

Printed in the United States of America.

ISBN 978-0-578-02163-8

Printed on acid-free paper.

Illustrations created by R. Berger & P. Sittivilai

Table of Contents

4

List of Figures

6

Chapter 1
General Orientation:
Psychology, Culture, and the
Audience

The celebrity is a person who is well-known for his well-knownness
Daniel Boorstin, (1962) *The Image*

On October 2, 1995 a seismic event took place. No, it was not a major catastrophic earthquake destroying entire cities, nor was it the outbreak of World War III and a nuclear holocaust. It was the rendering of the O. J. Simpson criminal trial. A reported 150 million viewers tuned in to see if Orenthal J. Simpson was found innocent or guilty of the murders of Nicole Brown Simpson and Ronald Lyle Goldman (Grace, 2005; Rantala, 1996; Schuetz, 1999). This high-profile court case is often reported as the most extensively covered media event in history (e.g., Furno-Lamude, 1999; Shaw, 1995; Schuetz, 1999). Clearly this media event occurred prior to the September 11, 2001 terrorist attacks or the start of the war in Iraq which, over time, will overshadow the attention and coverage of the Simpson trial. But the primary concern is: Why? Why all of the media coverage? Why were millions of Americans glued to their televisions during the unfolding case? Why have countless books, journal articles, and newspapers articles been written about this social and legal phenomenon?

Darden (1996) reported that the media system covering the O. J. Simpson criminal trial alone (not counting the later civil trial) included 19 televisions stations, 8 radio stations, 121 video feeds, 8 miles of cable, 850 telephones, 23 newspapers and magazines, and 2,000 reporters. *Why*? Not to trivialize the murder of two innocent victims, but people are murdered everyday in the United States and the general public barely, or in most cases never, hears a word about it. Why was this case so interesting to the masses? Why were so many people involved? Obviously there are many different factors to consider when answering these questions of "why" people watch (or read) celebrity court cases.

This book will focus primarily on the phenomena of *celebrity* in American culture, and how the various media feeds the audiences' needs and motives. The book will not set out to define what a celebrity is, how one is created by the media, and why people care about celebrities and their lives. A major focal point of the book is the attempt to better understand what a celebrity is, what makes one a celebrity, and what the media's role in it all is.

The mass media has fast become the central nervous system of modern American society. The average citizen spends most of their waking hours engaging some type of media form. Wahl (1995) argued that outside of working full-time nothing matches the hours spent watching television by most adults in the United States. Zillman (2000a) said that the reason people spend so much time in leisurely activities is because basic subsistence needs are now easily met for most people. He believed that this high level of spare time allows people to focus on emotional satisfactions and enjoyable activities. Shivers (1979) said that leisure means "a time of opportunity wherein the individual has the freedom to perceive and select experiences which are either worthwhile or simply gratifying" (p. 15). One could connect these thoughts to Abraham Maslow's (1943) hierarchy of needs where once basic human requirements are satisfied (i.e., food, shelter, clothing, safety from threat) people will pursue higher-level psychological hungers, such as creative endeavors and attachments.

Most leisure time is spent with media-related entertainment. Television is the number one source of societal entertainment, followed by (and in no particular order) the Internet, radio, books, magazines, video games, movies, and newspapers. To lay out some numbers, in a typical American home the television is on for more than 7 hours a day (and most homes now have more than one on at a time) (Comstock & Scharrer, 1999; Wahl, 1995). Dominick (1996) cited the circulation for daily newspapers at over 50 million, and that 400 million copies of magazines are purchased annually. Furno-Lamude (1999) said that the average person listens to the radio about 3 to 4 hours daily.

In our modern society, or "postmodern" if one follows the writings of many social philosophers (e.g., Michel Foucault, Jacques Lacan, Claude Levi-Strauss, Jean Baudrillard) that argue we now live in a world dominated by media images and mass consumption, it would make sense that the majority of people would seek psychological satisfactions in media presentations. This may explain why over 99% of all households have at least one television set (Comstock & Scharrer, 1999; Television Bureau of Advertising, 2005). If the previously stated statistics are to be believed then it makes sense to infer that all of this exposure is going to have deep-seated effects on both the micro and macro levels. Not only are individuals and small groups being influenced and affected by mediated events but the national culture at large has been, and is forever being, altered by print and electronic media. This paper is not about media effects per se (e.g., behavioral responses, physiologic reactions). This work is also indirectly interested in the psychological satisfactions and personal motivations that embrace media narratives. There is also an interest in the current effort that is concerned with how the producers of media narratives meet these aforementioned drives.

High-Profile

This book frequently uses the phrase "high-profile" to refer to the cases of interest. Although high-profile is not one of the central concepts being discussed in this presentation it is important to spell out to the reader what is meant by this phrase and what separates high-profile court cases from "ordinary" court cases. First, let it be understood that high-profile is referring to cases that are being covered by the major media and followed by the larger public. A case (or trial) that is well-known in a local town (e.g., Boise, Idaho) but is little or not known at all further away (e.g., Los Angeles, California) will not be considered a high-profile case. Even if an individual is popular in a local region but not outside of that territory it will still not be deemed high-profile for the purposes here. Grace (2005) made an interesting point. She says "every village and city has always had its own 'celebrities'—the wealthiest person in town, the mayor's wife, the high-school quarterback, the homecoming queen. There have always been those people, who for whatever reason fascinate other people" (p. 47). Even if the media are heavily covering a local "celebrity" trial it will still not be considered a high-profile case unless a wider audience is involved psychologically, and, as in most instances, socially with it.

Schuetz (1994) identified four characteristics of high-profile cases. (For the purposes of this paper let it be known that any time the word "case" is used it covers all legal matters whether criminal or not and all trials referenced. But not all cases are trials, (such as the Paris Hilton case). The first characteristic must involve persons, issues, or crimes of mass social interest. Examples mentioned in this study would include the Martha Stewart trial, the Michael Jackson trial, and the Winona Ryder trial. The second characteristic refers to extensive public interest and involvement. In this report the ratings and major media coverage will be the criteria by which to judge this. All of the cases discussed in this work will be supported by references to their popularity. Schuetz' third characteristic states that the case (trial) must make a contribution to the discourse regarding the legal system and the meaning of justice. As will be theorized, the notion of societal justice is a key ingredient as to why people watch these trials. The fourth characteristic is that these cases reflect the values of society in a contextual sense.

Audience Involvement

It is imperative to comprehend audience involvement and its role if we are to comprehend the phenomenon of celebrity and why it exists. It is also important to understand why involvement and attention are necessary for there to be any high-profile court cases at all. If the public has no involvement with a particular case and does not pay attention to it, the media would cease to cover the story and move on to another unfolding event. Recall, a case is only high-profile if high numbers of people are involved with it on some level. There is no numerical cut-off point but a case should be known by millions of people across the country. (This book is not attempting to make generalizations to a global audience due to difficulties in gathering data and inaccuracies in the statistics on ratings, coverage, etc. in foreign markets.)

One of the keys to how popular a case becomes depends on interest-involvement. Auter and Davis (1991) believed that interest-involvement stems from a person's behavioral and cognitive reactions to a stimulus; in this case a particular court case. They define involvement as "the level of cognitive processing a person performs and/or how much a person participates in a given activity" (p. 166). By this argument, the more interested a person is in a particular case the more involvement he or she will have in it. The more interest the more investment, the more investment the more involved a person will become. These components feed off of each other, reinforce one another, and propel the person to increasingly have more at stake psychologically. The determinants that spark audiences' interests are discussed at a later point.

Court cases perceived as involving or important to audience members leads to information processing. Perse (1990b) examined audience activity with television news. She found that higher cognitive and emotional involvement was positively correlated with strength of news viewing motivation and interest. Where does this motivation and interest come from? This will be addressed when discussing our celebrity-oriented culture and the relevant psychological typologies. But suffice it to say that involvement in court cases stems largely from central values and ego-involvement. Salmon (1986) said that if a topic activates core values a person becomes personally involved with the situation and thus reaffirms self-identity or one's self-picture. For example, if a person believes to her core that all violent criminals should be locked-up then she will naturally gravitate toward those high-profile cases in which the defendant is accused of a violent crime and thus reaffirm her core values and ego-involvement. If she fails to take notice of a violent criminal trial she may suffer a blow, however minor, to her self-concept.

Involvement is a psychological construct located within the particular individual, and is interpreted as an internal process or state (Wirth, 2006). This stance fits well with the approach being taken in this work. Why an individual will follow one case more than another, or follow no high-profile cases at all, should be fundamentally rooted in that individual's self-concept, ego-involvement, values, needs, and motives. Other authors have argued that involvement should be interpreted as a personality trait (e.g., Roser, 1990; Zaichkowsky, 1986) which could also be utilized to further develop the theoretical comprehension of this social phenomenon.

Involvement appears to be partitioned into four basic components by the leading scholars in this area. The first is the cognitive component which involves higher-order thinking processes, awareness, associations, learning, and comprehension (Cameron, 1993; Lo, 1994; Ray, 1973). Petty, Ostrom, and Brock (1981) lay the foundation for cognitive involvement by postulating that the cognitive response is determined by the extent to which the media narratives contain quality messages and deserve consideration. In other words, a media message that deserves consideration will stimulate the motivated individual to exert extensive and careful thoughts. Attention is also believed to be a core component of cognitive involvement and a prerequisite for its emergence (Greenwald & Leavitt, 1985; Perse, 1990b). Essentially, cognitive involvement is related to issue-oriented stimuli.

The second component of involvement is affective involvement. Park and McClung (1986) believed affective involvement relates to the subjective experience of mass-media usage. They believed that media involvement is most closely associated with emotions (e.g., excitement, fear, anger). As theorized, emotional involvement is a key component in regard to why people watch high-profile celebrity court cases. It is believed that emotional involvement and stimulation is a primary motive for the viewing audience.

The third component is conative involvement which encompasses action, behavior, and intention (Ray, 1973). According to Richins, Bloch, and McQuarrie (1992) conative involvement includes, active search for informative communication about experiences, and giving advice to others. Shoemaker, Schooler, and Danielson (1989) say that the conative component in regard to media usage is an indicator for behavioral involvement (e.g., how much, how long). When stressing the motivational side (and fourth component) of media involvement the viewer's intentions are emphasized (Slater, 2002).

Tania, a 22 year old college student:

Many admit it, and although some may not, the fact remains that our society is so absorbed with celebrities such as Lindsey Lohan, Britney Spears and other famous people, that it is almost everything that we talk about, everything that is discussed in mass media in general, and even creeps into our minds in the times that we are alone and are passively thinking or daydreaming in our unconscious states. Perhaps we may even have the experience of wishing to be like one of those ce;ebrities or having achieved some type of similarity with them. The effects of populariy and celebrities (those who we may call media and Hollywood personnel) are all standing and all in grossing [sic] because although from the distance, they have created an impact in our daily lives, our society, and our culture.

Chapter 2
" I Want to be Famous When I Grow Up"

Celebrity

There is no doubting that we live in a celebrity obsessed culture. Celebrities are highly paid, well-known, receive special treatment at hotels and restaurants, and are given free clothes and jewelry by the makers. In our modern day society celebrities are typical media ones. Evans and Wilson (1999) state that at least two-thirds of those we consider famous in our society come from the worlds of acting, singing, and other forms of entertainment. We tend to pay lip service to our Nobel Prize winners but how many people could identify and name them? The winners of the Oscars, Grammies, and Golden Globes are much more recognizable. In fact, in an article written by Dan Hurley (1988) he cited that some celebrities are recognized by over 90% of the public (e.g., Elvis Presley, Madonna, Oprah), and a 1985 *U.S. News and World Report* survey found that Clint Eastwood and Eddie Murphy were the top two heroes of young people.

But what is a celebrity and what function do they serve? Several studies have focused on the changes in American culture and values that now deems certain types worthy of celebrity status (e.g., Boorstin, 1962; Dyer, 1998; James, 1993). In contemporary American culture we seem to no longer "worship" the soldier, politician, or religious leader as much as the actor, dancer, and singer. The top rated shows on television by far are entertainment oriented (e.g., American Idol, Seinfeld). It is being postulated here that in a society where people "have it made," or at least in comparison to times past or impoverished nations, that people will tend to focus their energies toward more superficial, trivial, or entertainment endeavors. In other words, when people are starving they could not care less about who Jessica Simpson is dating or whether or not Paris Hilton is going to jail for driving under the influence of alcohol. As we, as a society, have become safer, more comfortable, more materialistic (as some sociologists have argued), and more leisurely, we focus our energies and interests more toward a different level of psychological needs not involving basic survival needs.

Celebrity refers to anybody that is well-known far beyond that of the average citizen. In essence, a celebrity is somebody that is famous. But how does one become famous? Evans and Wilson (1999) put it eloquently: "Some are born famous. Some work hard to achieve fame. Others have fame thrust upon them" (p. 45). These authors argue that in our society fame is the most sought after and prestigious social status one could achieve. Various authors believe that fame, in a sense, leads to almost god-like immortality (e.g., Marilyn Monroe, John Wayne, Elvis Presley). In a study focused on the worship of celebrities, Maltby, Houran, Lange, Ashe, and McCutcheon (2002) found that the psychological processes underlying the ways that celebrities are worshipped is significantly correlated with the ways people worship gods. Hurley (1988) says: "Fame in contemporary America has become a national obsession" (p. 53). Giles (2000), in his study on celebrity obsession, theorized that fame is a way to preserve oneself for eternity, and those that cannot themselves achieve fame can get one step closer psychologically by attaching themselves to a famous person. Mark Chapman, the man that shot and killed John Lennon, has been quoted as saying that he was not sure if he was going to kill Lennon or just get his autograph. Either way he wanted his name to go down in posterity with Lennon's.

In investigating how we choose our idols Stever (1991) conceived of four main categories that appeals to the audience: a) perceived sex appeal, b) perceived competence (talents, skills, power), c) prosocial qualities (trustworthiness, hardworking), and d) mystique (shyness, being misunderstood, mysterious). He found that Michael Jackson was so popular because of the public's perceptions pertaining to these four categories. It could be argued that most celebrities would rank high on at least two or three of Stever's (1991) categories. He went on to observe that people are attracted to celebrities because of their abilities to capture attention and entertain.

It will be shown throughout this work how the concept of celebrity and how the public feels about celebrities is a key factor in understanding why celebrity court cases are so popular. It is imperative that the reader grasps how the notions of celebrity and fame play into everything that is presented: This is a common thread interwoven throughout the conceptualization of this project that lures in and grabs the interest and attention of the audience.

Fame is a most valuable asset in our society, and celebrities are famous. We assume that simply because certain individuals have fame that they are somehow transcendent or extraordinary. We think, "They must be important because (after all) they're on television." It is being emphasized here to make the point that famous people can harness in and capture other's attention and involvement much more than the everyday citizen performing the same act can. "Dreams of the famous and the world they live in play at least as powerful a role in the formation of character as do our relationships with friends and family, our religion, and our place of origin" (Gross, 2005, p. 15). These dreams of the famous and their worlds are critical to comprehending why celebrity court cases are so engrossing to so many people.

This work focuses on those individuals that were famous prior to their entanglements with the law. (Exception: one of the most widely covered stories of 2007 involved the posthumous cases surrounding the Anna Nicole Smith saga.) There will be no distinction made between well-known celebrities such as Paris Hilton and Mel Gibson and what may be thought of as a quasi-celebrity such as Phil Spector and Michael Vick. If the individual was well-known in their respective fields (Phil Spector—music, Michael Vick—sports) and the media promotes them as celebrities, then they will be regarded as such. Individuals that were not known in any real or extensive way will not be regarded as a celebrity in an ensuing court case (such as Scott Peterson and Andrea Yates). Although these cases may be as extensively followed by the media and also garner high ratings, these individuals were popularized after the arrest (if criminal), or after the case was brought to court (other type of legal matter).

It is being acknowledged here that the media can create a celebrity out of just about any individual they want to. Given the right amount of press and coverage the media can thrust fame upon the ordinary citizen. If this was the case then these particular individuals should have attained this fame status prior to the legal cases. Nicole Richey and Paris Hilton are two stellar examples of famous individuals that have no real discernable talent but have become extremely popular and widely followed by the media and millions of interested starstruck fans.

Let it be stated at this point that any particular court case may also attract attention simply because of the counsel involved. It has been articulated in the various media that any court case will become a famous media case if certain high-profile attorneys are involved. Grace (2005) elucidated that any trial that involves well-known lawyers like the late Johnny Cochran, F. Lee Bailey, or Mark Garagos, will rise to the status of a celebrity court cases. These top-tiered lawyers, which includes several others like Tom Mesereau (Michael Jackson, Robert Blake), Robert Shapiro (O.J. Simpson), and Bruce Cutler (John Gotti, Phil Spector) will generate enough interest based on their prestige and status alone to elevate the defendant (if a criminal case) to some type of celebrity status—whether famous or infamous. These ongoing celebrity court cases will have most certainly been affected by the roles that the attorneys have played in elevating involvement in and attention toward their cases, both with viewers and the media.

To recap, viewers like to vicariously live out their lives through celebrities. This is not to say that people are transfixed with stars to the point of having a mental disturbance. It simply means, for whatever reasons, that celebrities seem to live fascinating lives. They are usually extraordinarily talented, charismatic, and/or attractive. If they are none of these things then this supports the statement made earlier about how the media can "make" anyone seem interesting and worth paying attention to.

Viewers (which from this point forward will also include readers; who view magazines, newspapers, and books) like to fantasize about celebrities and imagine themselves going through what the celebrities are going through. McCutcheon, Ashe, Houran, and Maltby (2003) discussed in their article on celebrity worship that it is a normal part of childhood, adolescence, and even adulthood to adore celebrities and see them as role models or idols. They say that celebrity adoration has an entertainment-social value that comprises both behaviors and attitudes of the audience members. This mentioned adoration may be thought of as a *symbolic attachment* to the media personality.

Feeling attached, or connected in some psychic or social way, to the celebrities in the mass media is believed to be a primary motive behind the popularity of the ongoing high-profile court cases in our society. These celebrity cases are covered in all forms of media from books, newspapers, and magazines, to the Internet and television. Blumler (1979) and Perse (1990b) believe that the print media are active, high-cognitive forms of media while the electronic forms are passive and low-cognitive. Whether these beliefs in cognitive energies are true or not the authors agree that both print and electronic forms of media serve the same attachment functions and equally meet psychological need and motives. The point being made here is that this paper will treat all forms of media as serving the same functions in the lives of the audience. The "audience" will be treated as a uniform whole not differentiating between book audiences, television audiences, etc. If a person is engaged in any way in an ongoing high-profile court case they will be referred to as the audience or viewer.

The celebrities detailed in this work are known largely through the electronic media. This is so because electronic media far outweighs print media in terms of how much time the average person in the United States spends with each. In review, the *Universal Almanac* (2000) calculates that over 100 million TV sets in the United States are turned on for over 7 hours a day. Robinson and Skill (1995) found that about 30% of the leisure time American adults have is spent watching television, which constitutes more than any other single activity.

Due to the enormity of studies conducted on (which if referenced would take up an entire book), and the statistics about how many hours a day people watch TV and the reported effects that this medium has, television will be treated as the current primary media form in society. Television will also be viewed as an active, engaging medium and not as a psychologically passive activity. For the purposes and argument of this paper to hold theoretical soundness the audience member must be assumed to be actively processing information and not just "zoning out" in front of the tube. This assumption will hold for all forms of media in relation to the study. As will be stressed later, following court cases is not something done with a shut off brain. The very nature of the law, the legal system, adversarial arguments, guilt or innocence, and weighing evidence demands high-level cognitive processing on the viewer's part. This holds regardless of the medium being utilized by any particular audience member.

Hillary, a 43 year old immigrant:

> *Three years ago I moved to the United States, and ever since then all I ever hear and see on the television is news about some celebrity.*

Drama

One of the most fundamental appeals to watching the unfolding of a high-profile court case is its inherent drama. Celebrity court cases tend to have all of the twists and turns, action, suspense, and interesting players that would be found in a good Hollywood movie. *Merriam-Webster* (2003) defined drama as "a state, situation, or series of events involving interesting or intense conflict of forces" (p. 378). Drama is all about conflict, and conflict is what makes celebrity court cases exciting to watch. In a celebrity trial the prosecution is in constant battle with the defense. The prosecutors pound the defense witnesses, while the defense lawyers do the same to the witnesses for the prosecution. The judge is often in conflict with both sides by trying to maintain a fair and controlled courtroom. Often the families and friends of the victims (or plaintiffs) are in conflict with the family and friends of the defendant. Even the various media outlets are in conflict with one another over getting the best scoop, presenting the best story, and getting the highest ratings.

The first social thinker to really articulate the appeal of drama was Aristotle. He believed that it was natural for people to want to watch tragedies because human beings are naturally geared toward conflict and resolution. Scheff (1979) said that Aristotle believed that people seek aversive experiences through tragedy and find relief afterward. Thus, the resolution of drama leads from a distressing emotional state to residual excitation leading to a subsequent euphoric emotional state. Put another way, at the end of a tragedy the audience switches from distress to euphoria and leaves the drama in a positive emotional state.

Media producers have long understood this need of the audience. Almost all television shows and motion pictures follow the same "arc" whether it be a comedy or drama. Zillman (2000b) believed that comedy is a form of drama because it not only dwells on conflict and its resolution, but also because it entails the essential plots that characterize drama. The "plots" seen in drama includes three basic acts: the introduction (becoming familiar with plot and characters), the conflict (battle between opposing forces), and the resolution (closure). It has been shown through the box office that audiences do not like to leave the theatre feeling as though the story is not finished and that there was no closure.

Aristotle elaborated on two conditions that make for enjoyable drama. First, he stated that "a good man must not be seen passing from happiness to misery," and second, "a bad man from misery to happiness" (trans. 1966). In other words, any miscarriage of justice, whether it is a good person being wronged or a bad person gaining fortune, is distressing and not enjoyable to the audience. "The gospel of enjoyable drama is that, first, good persons must improve their lot in life and gain incentives; and second, bad persons must experience a deterioration of their fortunes and suffer due punishment" (Zillman, 2000b, p. 38). Hollywood producers have long understood this statement. It is unofficial knowledge that any movie which ends with a miscarriage of justice will immediately lose at least 20% of the box office revenue.

Much like the recipient of a manufactured dramatic presentation, the viewer of a high-profile court case wants to see the good guy win and the bad guy lose. Media covered court cases amplifies the conflict and adds creative dramatic elements that delivers in such a way that heightens emotions and escalates action (Schultze, 1991). A case in point was the dramatic lure of the O.J. Simpson "trial of the century." The Simpson trial was unprecedentedly followed in the media from the very beginning of the case, through to the verdict, and continued on post-verdict. Uelman (1996) penned that the Simpson case had all the ingredients of a great drama. It had celebrity, charismatic and memorable characters, murder, and to top it off, television cameras in the courtroom. He said that adding the cameras was "like throwing gasoline on a fire, it transformed the proceedings into a sort of 'hype heaven'" (p. 94).

As the dramatic elements increase in a celebrity court case so does its entertainment appeal, and thus becomes more of a major news event or spectacle. The Simpson case had all of the elements of a national media event (Bloom, 1996). Surette (1989) defined a "media trial" as a major media event in which the media use the criminal justice system as a source of high drama and entertainment. It becomes, in essence, a miniseries built around a real criminal case. As will be purported throughout the thesis at hand, all celebrity court cases have inherent dramatic appeal. This innate interest is then captured by and intensified within the strategically presented media depictions.

Suspense is one of the most important elements of drama. It is suspense that peaks our interest, keeps us involved, plays on our worst fears, and gives us cathartic relief. Brewer (1996) said that suspense even supersedes conflict in terms of emotional response to witnessing dramatic events. It is the suspense that leaves the viewer wondering "what is going to happen?" Vorderer and Knobloch (2000) believed that the main questions raised by witnessing dramatic events are rooted in the suspense that is generated by the plot. They say that suspense, from a psychological point of view, is primarily an affective and cognitive experience of media users, and that this is a primary psychological motivation for seeking suspense in the first place.

The more intense the suspense is, the better the drama. The higher the suspense is the higher cognitive and affective involvement. According to Perse (1990a), the two primary motivations for watching television news is enjoyment and drama. It is being argued here that without conflict there is no suspense, with no suspense there is no drama, thus there is little or no enjoyment. Think about the 150 million Americans that were glued to their televisions on October 2, 1995 to hear the verdict in the Simpson murder trial. This moment was suspense at its highest possible level. This was the end of the third act, the resolution. And this is why so many people were involved: "What was going to happen?"

The comprehension of the role that suspense and drama play's in motivating viewers to watch high-profile court cases is imperative. The stance being taken here is that all high-profile celebrity court cases contain intrinsic elements of drama and suspense. These elements are then heightened and blown-up by the media to further capture attention and interest. Once in motion the audience will continue to follow these cases and the media will continue to construct these plots in a strategic fashion. This will happen all the way up to the point of resolution at the end of the third act where suspense (and interest and enjoyment) is at its peak, the verdict is rendered, and the drama (in theory) comes to an end. (Although the media will frequently continue to prolong the conflict as long as it is profitable to do so.)

Tania, a 25 year old hair stylist:

> *It is only natural for our culture to be obsessed with the lives of celebrities, especially if one lives in Los Angeles. We watch celebrities in movies and on television, and chances are we may have seen a few of them in the streets of Hollywood, Beverly Hills, or even the Valley...We are on the look out [sic] for them...When we see celebrities on the streets going about their business it seems they are like us. Except for two big things, they are famous and most likely rich.*

Chapter 3
"Resistance is Futile"
The Borg

Media's Role

High-profile celebrity court cases do not just appear out of thin air. The various mediums systematically set up, package, and transmit the images and stories they want you to see and how they want you to see them. These narratives aid in constructing how people understand and make sense of their worlds. Audiences rely on "a version of reality built from personal experience, interaction with peers, and interpreted selections from the mass media" (Neuman, Just, & Crigler, 1992, p. 120). These interpretations are meant to satisfy the psychological needs discussed in this work. Stated differently, the audience has needs and wants, and these needs and wants are purposefully being nourished by media producers.

Celebrity court cases are media created events. It is the various forms of communication that allows millions of Americans to view these legal entanglements from a safe, convenient place. High-profile court cases are a part of the news and according to Epstein (2000) television is the chief source of news for most of Americans. He also stated that television is the most believable source of news for most of the population. In Epstein's seminal work *News from Nowhere* he argues that all news, especially television news, is a manufactured product created by complex organizational structures. It is the television networks taken as a bureaucratic whole that ultimately determines what makes it to the airwaves. It is not the biases or interests of reporters or other news personnel. Ultimately, it is the larger corporate organizations that decide on which pictures of society will be represented on television as national news (Epstein, 2000).

The major media are big business. Their goal is to generate stories that titillate public interest and satisfy social and psychological needs. According to Epstein (2000), what determines whether or not an event will be covered is its "newsworthiness," which is usually encircled around the question "who is involved?" Epstein found that public figures like politicians, actors, and athletes usually are the most newsworthy. In his work all of the public figures could be labeled as celebrities, and thus, by default, when any celebrity gets caught up in a legal case it is almost automatically newsworthy. The media are out for ratings, or sales. A newsworthy news event like a celebrity court case can virtually guarantee public interest and thus revenue.

On June 17, 1994 the three major news networks (ABC, CBS, NBC) and the top cable news network (CNN) all interrupted their regular programming to go to the live television coverage of a police chase in Los Angeles, California of a white Ford Bronco. On this day, 95 million people viewed this chase with the suspense of not knowing how it was going to end (Furno-Lamude, 1999; Nielsen, 1994). A police chase is interesting, but a police chase involving a celebrity murder suspect is almost too much to be able to ignore. The intrigue generated from an event such as this is almost perfect sustenance for the public's psychological hungers. This satisfaction can easily be inferred from the ratings and coverage, which only heightened after the Bronco chase.

The coverage of the media in the O.J. Simpson case can only be speculated on as it was an event too widely covered to be known for certain. Some of the reported statistics give a hint: *Newsweek* magazine published six cover stories about the Simpson trial in a 10-month period; more than 1,000 stories on the case were published in major newspapers alone in the 16 months after the murders ("*The Simpson Legacy*," 1995, October 9, p. S4); and the endless hours devoted to the trial on television where shows like CNBC's *Rivera Live* and Court TV (now called Tru TV) devoted the great majority if its time to its coverage (Rantala, 1996).

This mass coverage of a social event is a conscious effort by the media to influence the general collective consciousness of people in a society to orient them and guide them toward becoming mass consumers in a media culture (Fishman, 1980; Snow, 1983). This is not to say that the public is not a thinking mass, but what it is saying is that the media, with its pervasive and omnipresent influence, can shape perceptions, values, and interests. Snow's (1983) main thesis is that prior to this media influence being able to take effect, "the audience must willingly participate and willingly accept the perspectives and content presented through mass media. Media influence occurs when people begin to see and define their environment as the mass media see and define it" (p. 30). For example, the public has psychological needs and motives which, from a social and evolutionary perspective, automatically cause them to pay attention to some conflict in society such as the O. J. Simpson Bronco chase. The media takes advantage of these opportunities by covering the stories in a fashioned way thereby furthering the public interest. The public accepts this willingly and both sides win out.

In discussing media use and its influence, Snow (1983) believed that to be able to understand the development of media influence and media culture one needs to see the interaction between the audience and the communicator where "both parties use perspectives and grammatical rules to perceive and interpret various phenomena" (p. 27). He additionally believed that the particular motives for using these grammatical forms and perspectives lie with the audience members. His model on the relationship between both media communicator and audience member entails four distinct usages: a) mass media is a source of information on subjects of relevance to the two interacting parties; b) mass media provide information on the perspectives that underlie why the audience should care about a subject and how to respond; c) mass media are used by audience members as a source of trusted and credible information, and d) vicarious and overt interaction networks exist within and between the media industry and between the audience members and the medium.

The dynamic interplay between the image creators and the audience is a focal point of this project's conceptualization. How do the media serve the needs of the viewers? How do the creators disseminate high-profile court case information in such a way that continually re-motivates the viewers to keep watching or reading about the ongoing stories? In media trials, one of the keys to this ongoing motivation to watch is access of the media. Furno-Lamude (1999) stated that, "In order for a news story to become a spectacle, the trial judge must permit television cameras in the courtroom" (p. 30). In other words, without media access to what is happening inside the courtroom an O. J. Simpson debacle could have never taken place. In fact, no cameras were allowed to cover any celebrity court case gavel-to-gavel from inside the courtroom in Los Angeles from the rendering of the verdict in the O. J. Simpson murder trial in 1995 up until 2007 when trial judge Larry Fidler gave the green light for Tru (Court) TV to air the Phil Spector murder trial.

This "telelitigation," as Schuetz (1999) put it, allows the cameras to emphasize personality and stardom of key players (e.g., celebrity lawyers and defendants), create dramatic portrayals (which boost ratings), direct attention to feeling rather than argumentation, and reinforce faith and credibility to communication technology. Schuetz (1999) held that telelitigation is simply a means to satisfy the public's desire to have massive amounts of information about celebrity cases. Tru TV agrees with this statement. In a position paper they explain their mission in following legal cases:

> Television coverage of trials tells the whole, real, true story about a complicated, often misunderstood and under reported subject. It allows the participants in a democracy to judge for themselves how well the government institution that makes the most fundamental decision that any government makes—liberty or prison—is working. (Quoted in Caplan, 1996, p. 203)

Understanding how the media selects, frames, and delivers the images and narratives the audience receives is an important part of this study. Although it is not a part of the psychological model presented in a later chapter it is one side of this media and viewer equation and thus must be addressed. Recall, the viewers have various needs and motives. These needs and motives are fed and stimulated heavily by media portrayals, content, and structure. It is not one-sided. It is a dynamic give-and-take between the producers who mediate court case litigation and conflict and the consumers of this telelitigated drama.

Brief Summary

The purpose thus far has been to explain and discuss what constitutes a high-profile celebrity court case, why people care and participate in the ongoing drama of these cases, the key players, and the media's role in the equation. I have begun to introduce some of the fundamental psychological needs and motivations of the viewing audience, along with how these needs and motives are being met by strategically packaged media content and presentation. There is a synergy between the audience and producers. They both need and feed off of each other for mutual gain. Understanding this basic equation is the first step in conceptually grasping why celebrity court cases are so popular with the viewing audience and so widely covered by the media communicators.

We are a culture of celebrity watchers and media consumers. Moulton and O'Connor (2006) declared that ever since the O. J. Simpson trial whenever a famous person is charged with a crime that two trials take place. One of the trials is in the courtroom and the other is in the media. This includes both how the manufacturers present it and how the viewers interpret and make judgments about it.

A good example of how this works is the Martha Stewart obstruction of justice trial. Stewart was a syndicated TV show host, magazine owner, and finer living entrepreneur worth over $1 billion. When her day in court arrived the coverage was not focused on her innocence or guilt, but on the Birkin by Hermes purse she was carrying which typically run from $6,000 to $85,000 each. This image of the mogul was interpreted in the media, and thus largely by the viewing audience, as a slap in the face of the common American. It was if she was saying she was a member of the elite privileged class and this was not taken well by the public. American sentiment shifted more toward wanting to see her get prosecuted and brought down to size. Stewart's troubles were exacerbated after she decided to show up on another day wearing a fur ascot (that she claims was faux) that the media jumped all over causing more damage to her public approval ratings (Moulton & O'Connor, 2006). On March 5, 2004 after 6 weeks of trial and 3 days of deliberation Stewart was found guilty on all four counts laid by the U.S. Attorney's office.

Why does the public seem to care so much? Why are they so interested in these court cases? One reason is familiarity. Stever (as cited in Fischoff, 1996) argued that celebrities are familiar rather than strangers to the public. He says that even though this familiarity is not firsthand it does cause people to take an interest in their lives, even if it is mediated familiarity. Often times this familiarity is successfully manufactured in the media thus creating a positive halo effect influencing future judgments and inferences about a celebrity's guilt or innocence (Mitroff & Bennis, 1989). This halo effect crosses over into audience perceptions about the celebrity's dispositions and overall character traits. This may help explain why so many people refused to believe that adored Heisman trophy winner, NFL star, and movie actor could have possibly committed a heinous double murder, even in the face of such overwhelming evidence. Either way, celebrity seems to be perceived as part of an individual's context of personality traits which serves to connect the famous person to the audience member (Fischoff, 1996).

Whatever the exact reasons are, people have always seemed to be fascinated with famous individuals; those who can set themselves apart from the herd. Whether it be an honored battlefield warrior in days past, a member of Shakespeare's acting company, or a modern day media personality, people have always been drawn to the members of their societies that stand out and do something "bigger" than the average citizen will ever do. Fame, familiarity, fantasy, attraction, immortality, and many more factors all appear to contribute to our fascination with the lives of celebrities. This public fascination is only intensified when a famous person finds himself or herself caught up in a widely covered, dramatic legal entanglement.

Alberto, a 42 year old accountant:

Celebrity court cases are mostly covered for the simple fact that they are popular figures. They already have a fan following, it's understandable that the media would want to take advantage of their fan base. The media is very smart in taking advantage of people and their interest for celebrities.

Nikki, a 37 year old financial officer:

Celebrity court cases are interesting because they show us that celebrities are human and subject to the same laws that we are. They are like soap operas; there are specific characters such as the celebrity and his or her attorney or attorneys, the deliberations are shown daily, and we get addicted to them. Sometimes we have life experiences that are similar, and we are curious about the treatment a celebrity will receive compared to our own or others we know. We may even be fans of the attorneys, and wonder how they can get someone out of a legal mess.

Jim, a 24 year old undergraduate:

Compared to the average person celebrities have almost everything, money, friends, popularity, and much more. People become jealous and envious of the power or fame celebrity posses [sic]...Celebrities live a life that the average person can only dream of, but never posses unless they themselves become a celebrity.

Chapter 4
The Action is Parasocial

In order to be a member in good standing in American society, one should possess
information about people one has never actually met.
J. Caughey, (1984) *Imaginary Social Worlds*

Parasocial Interaction

The media-related survey instrument being employed for this project incorporates a number of established theories and concepts that were primarily conceived of in social and media psychological studies. The most prominent scholars and works are discussed in this chapter to disseminate the knowledge that is necessary to comprehend the nature and relevance of the instrument presented later in this work. This chapter presents, in some detail, each single theoretical "tree" in a separated, isolated context, after which, the effort pulls all theories together to present the entire conceptual "forest." To be able to grasp this multi-component psychological forest one must first be cognizant of each individual theoretical tree, and how each single tree contributes to the overall portrait being presented. Rest assured, there is some psychological play between the theories, much like some mental illnesses are comorbid and highly correlated. But before one can run one must learn to walk. It is believed here that understanding the basics first will be invaluable in assisting the reader in having a deeper comprehension of the ensuing study, and will also aid in forming a critical evaluation of its potential merit and contribution.

The overarching objective of this literature review is to bring forth the sensitizing concepts and fundamental theories being promulgated and supported in this work. The goal is to disseminate the pertinent media psychological theories that are grounded in the prevailing literature and to convey to the reader how each unique theory contributes to our better understanding of the topic at hand. Each of the distinguishable theories and concepts are initially treated as independent aspects that make up the larger theoretical picture. This literature review should assist in bringing an understanding of how the survey instrument (which will be introduced in a later chapter) was created and also give order to its rationale. It may be helpful to think of the various theories independently at first. This approach may aid in helping one to have a more thorough comprehension of how these theories first function separately (considering them one at a time), and then ultimately how they may function together serving the viewer's needs and motivations. Think of the components in this literature review as being put together in a fragmentary way, one step at a time. It is a piecemeal work that hopes to establish a contributing theoretical baseline that has some applicability and will aid in comprehending the cultural phenomenon of media covered celebrity court cases.

Robert, a 28 year old math teacher:

Celebrity activity is everywhere. No matter what channel you tune the TV to or what radio station you listen to or what publication you pick up, celebrity happenings are forced on us. You can't get away from seeing or hearing what celebrities are doing. It could be as mundane as where someone went shopping the day before to something as serious as a murder trial. No matter what the scenario, celebrity information has become a large part of our media coverage.

Parasocial Interaction

Figure 1. Illustration of parasocial interaction (PSI) with the media celebrity.

Many studies have focused on the apparent "relationships" that often form between a celebrity and a fan (e.g., Cohen, 2004; Giles & Maltby, 2004; Vorderer, 1996). It is believed in these studies that as people watch a specific person, or persons, over and over again across time that they eventually come to feel that they actually "know" the celebrity personally and also come to believe that they, on some level, are involved in these same celebrity's lives. The psychology of these feelings of the audience member has been the focus of an eclectic abundance of research from the 1950s to the present. This fascinating area of inquiry is still proving to be a valuable conceptualization of the psychology between the viewer and the media personality.

The seminal work in parasocial interaction (PSI) was created by Horton and Wohl (1956). In this effort they conceived of the idea that new media technologies (television, radio, movies) give the illusion that the spectator has a real face-to-face relationship with the media personality. They argued that this illusory relationship occurs for several reasons. The first reason is because the "actor" is seen engaged with others in what appears to be a real dialogue and this pulls the spectator into the belief he or she is watching a true drama unfolding. A second reason that PSI takes place is because the actor often faces the spectator and converses directly and privately to him or her thus increasing the viewer's involvement. A third and powerful reason that PSI takes place is the ongoing "intimacy" that viewers have with the media personality. The media persona offers a continuous relationship that is regular, dependable, and thus becomes integrated into the routines of the spectator's daily lives.

Horton and Wohl (1956) penned that although the interaction is characteristically one-sided, not susceptible to mutual development, nondialectical, controlled by the performer, and built around fantasy, the audience member nevertheless forms a sense of personal obligation to the performer. With this sense of obligation the viewer makes sure that he or she is home at the proper times so as to not miss an episode and violate the "trust" in the relationship. The audience member will support the performer's "successes" and sympathize or "fight" for the "nonsuccesses." This spectator support is fundamentally derived from the peculiar similarities between the social situations the media persona establish for their audiences and real-life social encounters. With this, they argue that viewers ultimately wind up establishing a quasi-relationship with media personalities over time which increases in importance to the viewer's actual social life.

Ruth, a 36 year old social worker:

I found that there are three reasons why I like to watch celebrity news. The first being just to pass time when there is nothing else to watch on TV and when I am waiting in line at the supermarket. Another was because I like to answer back to the television. I often believe that I know more than the people who are on the television giving their opinions on the stars. Lastly, I watch just so that I know the gossip.

Why does this parasocial interaction occur in the first place? Horton and Wohl (1956) believed it is an opportunity for the spectator to live out roles he or she would otherwise not ever have. They believed that PSI is compensatory in nature and allows opportunities that would have otherwise never presented themselves in ones social environment. They said: "This function of the para-social then can properly be called compensatory, inasmuch as it provides the socially and psychologically isolated with a chance to enjoy the elixir of sociability" (p. 222). With this compensatory attachment the illusion of a personal and intimate relationship has been established. Although Horton and Wohl (1956) looked toward the socially inept, the aged, the rejected, the invalid, and the timid in explaining PSI, more contemporary social scientists believe that PSI can, and does, occur in healthy, normally functioning children and adults not lacking in social relationships (e.g., Klimmt, 2003; Klimmt, Hartmann, & Schramm, 2006; Lee, 2004).

Parasocial interaction is believed to be analogous to social interaction in ordinary primary groups. In a society dominated by media imagery people may become "familiar" with more people parasocially than directly through face-to-face contact. Through this familiarity media spectators form beliefs and attitudes about real individuals (e.g., athletes, politicians) and fictional characters, but rarely do they make a distinction between the two (Auter & Palmgreen, 2000). Why do viewers usually not make this distinction? R. B. Rubin and M. Rubin (2001) wrote that PSI is "grounded in interpersonal notions of attraction, perceived similarity or homophily, and empathy" (p. 326). The belief is that viewers use the same social communication and cognitive processes for both real and mediated encounters. Perse and R.B. Rubin (1989) said that "people and media are coequal communication alternatives that satisfy similar communication needs and provide similar gratifications" (p. 59).

Michelle, a 52 year old college counselor:

> *In our society we are continually bombarded with celebrities in the media, whether it is on television, on the radio, or in the newspapers. In the United States, especially, we seem to be obsessed with celebrities and there [sic] everyday movements. The media is something that is quite hard to get away from seeing as how we are continually surrounded by its images and portrayals of celebrities. Often times we compare ourselves to these images we see in the media, which is becoming [sic] to pose quite a problem.*

Conway and A. M. Rubin (1991) wax that in "real life" people form positive or negative attitudes toward other people, and such is the case when viewers watch characters on television. They believe that with this parasocial response to media personalities arises a one-sided parasocial interaction. With this said parasocial response can come feelings of friendship, affinity, interest, imitation, liking, or identification (Giles, 2002; R.B. Rubin & M. Rubin, 2001). This parasocial response may also lead to the opposite feelings of disdain, rejection, dislike, lack of identification, or lack of friendship and empathy. This can be witnessed in cases where the viewer yells at a character on TV, feels good when a disliked character suffers, or roots for her liked character to beat her disliked character. In other words, it is possible to interact with a media personality even when that personality is viewed negatively.

Kanazawa (2002) said that the human brain processes media experience in much the same manner that it processes "direct experience," and that people typically react to televised characters as they would people in actual life. He believed that people's cognitive responses are basically the same in regard to mediated versus real life experiences. Reeves and Nass (1996) agreed with this and also include equivalent responses in the viewer to the mediated versus real world comparison. The fundamental belief is that mediated presentations are close enough to real life in terms of familiarity, character relationships, drama, suspense, etc. that it stirs up the same affective responses in the viewers, becomes implanted in their cognitions, and thus becomes a part of their "real" lives.

What factors contribute to PSI? As with real life interactions, the media personalities usually carry some level of similarity to the affected viewer, exhibit character traits admired by the viewer, are involved in something important or interesting to the viewer, and/or are attractive (physically, socially, functionally) to the viewer (Caughey, 1986; Cohen, 2001; Turner, 1993; Visscher & Vorderer, 1998). Gender and age also appear to be factors contributing to viewer PSI (Gleich, 1997; Levy, 1979; Vorderer, 1996). R. B. Rubin and M. Rubin (2001) believed that PSI is largely grounded in empathy toward the media persona. Cohen (2001) suggested that empathy and homophily creates the basic attraction that is the foundation of PSI.

What types of media programs are best suited for PSI? Are certain types of programs more likely to foster PSI over other types (forms, genres) of programs? Most researchers in this area believe that television is the most powerful force in creating parasocial interactions with the viewers, followed by radio, then newspapers and movies. Nordlund (1978) believed that television has the highest PSI potential because of its recurring characters. Television dramas, soaps, newscasts, or sitcoms occur on a regular basis so the viewer can plan his or her schedule around these times and days which, in turn, creates a pseudo-bonding with the media persona. As PSI develops with television personalities, which is due to repeated exposure and mediated effects, connections develop over time where empathy increases, uncertainty is reduced, intimacy grows, and reliance on the character is strengthened (Conway & A. M. Rubin, 1991; Gibbons, Vogl, & Grimes, 2003; Levy, 1979). A. M. Rubin, Perse, and Powell (1985) noted that viewers tend to want to become a part of the social world the media personalities are in and will familiarize themselves increasingly with the personas behaviors, attitudes, appearances, and styles. As this increasing familiarity builds and strengthens over time through repeated exposure so does the relationship between spectator and media persona.

Television celebrities will often adopt a conversational style with the audience that exudes warmth and thus promotes a pseudo-friendship with the viewer (Bogart, 1980; Powers, 1978). Giles (2000) has written about the intentional design in television presentations by studio executives to foster parasocial relationships. The belief is that those most susceptible to strong PSI attachment and thus loyalty to the programs are those that experience loneliness and/or shyness. Shyness refers to discomfort and inhibition while around others (Cheek & Buss, 1981), and shy persons tend to have few friends, unsatisfactory interpersonal involvements, talk less, and are often viewed as unfriendly (Jones & Russell, 1982). Perse and A. M. Rubin (1990) defined loneliness as a persistent sense of isolation over time. Spitzberg and Canary (1985) believed that lonely people lack communication skills and this furthers their social isolation. Jones, Rose, and Russell (1990) found that shyness and loneliness are two closely related constructs that have a typical correlate of .40 to .50. Thus, when attempting to understand the ways in which PSI can occur, being aware of a particular individual's social skills, extraversion, confidence, and social networks, or conversely shyness and loneliness, is an aid in explaining why some people may turn to media when seeking gratifications. According to Ashe and McCutcheon (2001) shy and lonely people are more attracted to parasocial relationships because they make few social demands (friendliness, communication) and eliminate the discomfort felt when in the presence of real people.

Parasocial interaction can occur with newscasters presenting the stories of the day. Newscasters are prime targets for PSI because of their consistent nature. They dress in a familiar, recognizable fashion, they appear at predictable and regular times, and they speak with a consistent tone, pitch, and rhythm. Watching television news has been shown to be a highly social activity which fosters mediated surrogate friendships (Perse, 1990b). Because of this, the interaction between television news personalities and the news audience is a prime spot to investigate the phenomenon of parasocial interaction.

Levy (1979) believed that those most likely to bond with a newscaster are people with weak social ties and the elderly. He posited that PSI offers a useful alternative for unsatisfactory interpersonal relationships. In explaining the dominant functions of PSI and why it occurs, Levy (1979) discussed the relations experienced between the audience and newscaster:

> First and foremost, the para-social relationship is based on an affective tie which many members of the audience create with the communicators. Even though this affective tie is completely the subjective invention of the audience, para-socially interactive viewers believe it is genuine and they interpret the behavior of the news personae as reciprocating this "real" bond....People who engage in para-social interaction are often reassured by a familiar, friendly "image" of their intimates-at-a-distance; and para-socially active viewers experience a sense of order, belonging, and context from their relationship with the news personae. (p. 78)

Levy (1979) continues on to explain that a primary motive for bonding with newscasters revolves around friendship and trust. Audience members want to feel secure and comfortable with the television personalities that enter their homes on a regular basis. These aforementioned motivations will serve as a key factor in the model developed in a later chapter.

Why do viewers become so involved with media personalities? Why do viewers become so involved in the unfolding of a celebrity court case? Do newscasters play a role in stimulating interest in watching these high-profile legal disputes? The answers to these questions have not been directly addressed in research on parasocial interaction but some studies have given hints. Perse (1990a) said that there are three reasons why PSI grows out of information seeking in news. First, viewers come to be acquainted with the actual news personality. Berger and Calabrese (1975) posited that interpersonal knowledge is an important antecedent to relationship development. Second, newscasters help the viewers meet their needs. McCain, Chilberg, and Wakshage (1977) said that those who give us information we seek will be perceived more favorably. Third, newscasters tend to be dynamic, sociable, and extraverted, all of which build on credibility and positive viewer perceptions.

Perse (1990a) also argued that PSI is linked to news viewing attitudes and behaviors that indicate higher levels of involvement. This involvement will hold regardless of the medium employed. In other words, if a viewer is getting her news from television, radio, or newspaper, the level of cognitive involvement should be the same because it is all based around information-seeking and need fulfillment. PSI can occur with any medium, although television, by its impacting visual and audio nature, seems to produce the strongest "relationships." Perse (1990a) summarized PSI with television news by stating that, "Higher levels of parasocial interaction, then, should be associated with: (a) an informational orientation toward television news, (b) cognitive involvement with local news, (c) emotional involvement with the news" (p. 22). It is believed here that viewing high-profile celebrity court cases entails these stated components of information-seeking, cognitive involvement, and emotional involvement. These components then provide the seeds that nourish a strong parasocial involvement with celebrity court cases and the newscasters that present them.

Parasocial interaction appears to be one of the most important viewing motives of news audiences. The interaction patterns between the audiences and news anchors provide a basis for personalized and emotional offerings (Bente & Vorderer, 1997). It is believed that PSI largely occurs because of the presentational format of direct form of address (toward the audience) and related communicative acts (Foltin, 1994; Schumacher, 1992; Sullivan, 1991). News anchors speak directly to the audience which mimics real-life interaction and thus creates similar emotional attachments and likings. Anchorpersons also tend to reveal their personalities (Court TV, which, again, is now named Tru TV, is a prime example) and not act like mindless robots, which further encourages psychological symbolic interaction.

Jacob, a 31 year old lawyer:

> *I turn on the TV and watch the news mainly Good Day L. A. with Gillian Barberie, Steve Edwards, and Dorothy Lucy. These people make it very fun to listen to the news, they are not very serious, and the reason I watch them specifically is because they are usually always arguing with each other. This makes it very interesting for me because it fulfills my boredom and kills time when I have nothing to do. After a while of watching it became more of an addiction, usually a morning doesn't go by and I don't watch their show. They usually talk about celebrity court cases and they always have their own two cents about the celebrity and what they did wrong. If I had to say anything about how their show motivates me it would be that they make me feel like I am one of them, and usually I compare myself or other people to the stars.*

If PSI develops over time with repeated viewing of a television personality then it seems natural that news anchors would be prime targets for this psychological attachment. Perse and R. B. Rubin (1989) stated that deeper feelings about media persona come only after the audience member has been exposed to a number of parasocial encounters and thereby gains attributional confidence about the persona. Although this "interaction" with news casters is one-sided it appears to satisfy several gratifications and motives in viewers. McGuire (1974) argued that interaction with media personalities fulfills expressive and affiliation needs. Rosengren (1974) felt that involvement with television characters serves as a "consumption relationship" where the audience member temporarily meets connective needs. News personalities covering celebrity court cases are prime targets to meet these various needs and motivations of the spectator.

It is argued here that the entire "scene" of a celebrity court case lends itself to audience PSI. Celebrity cases tend to be covered in the media almost everyday (if not *every* day, throughout the day), have regular players, and highly encourage viewer involvement. The newscasters giving the play-by-play, the celebrity defendant (if criminal), the prosecuting and defense attorneys, and even the judge (e.g., Larry Fidler, Lance Ito) can all play into the eventual parasocial interaction, interest, and involvement of the audience member. All of the characters in a court case act together to sort of form a theatric ensemble which, as is being argued here, serves to foster a strong, eclectic PSI involvement in the unfolding legal drama. The fact that the main player - the celebrity defendant - is already well-known only strengthens the PSI bond and viewer commitment.

Parasocial interaction has not yet been investigated with a celebrity defendant but there is no reason to assume that it would have any less of an appeal to the viewer than the news anchor discussing the case. The celebrity is in the courtroom everyday; his or her appearance, gait, and demeanor is discussed continually; and everything attainable about the celebrity's life (past and present) is uncovered, gossiped about, critiqued, and disseminated to the audience member. It can be inferred with all of this that PSI with a celebrity defendant would almost be a certainty with involved viewers. All of the factors that foster PSI are present in a highly covered celebrity court case.

Kevin, a 25 year old marketer:

> *When Scott Peterson was convicted, I was working at a law firm, watching all the lawyers critiquing and analyzing his sentencing. The interesting part about it was that Scott Peterson was not really a celebrity, not until the media made him become the main "stream issue." On the other hand, when Paris Hilton was arrested and sentenced for 30 days in jail, I was in summer school and the professor and the students talked about it daily. So I think that people, especially students, might see it to there [sic] advantage to watch or read famous trials. It enables individuals to relate it to there [sic] current subjects of interest.*

Attachment Theory and PSI

A strong determinate as to whether or not one forms a parasocial relationship with a media persona is how attached they become to the players in the drama. Viewers of celebrity court cases may themselves become emotionally attached to the celebrity's lives and thus more involved in the case outcome than they would be in an average citizen's legal entanglement. The viewer may also find himself or herself attached to other key players in the case (lawyers, judges, expert witnesses, media commentators, news persona) further deepening parasocial involvement with the entire cast. What should be stated here is that PSI does not have to just revolve around the celebrity on trial. PSI can potentially involve any courtside personality catching media attention and viewer involvement. Although the celebrity is the central figure in the case, PSI may potentially run deeper with another courtroom player or with any media newsperson covering the case with any particular viewer.

Attachment theory is based on the work of John Bowlby (1973, 1982, 1988). He believed that attachments formed (or not formed) during childhood have a significant impact on an individual's adult relationships and attachments. Bolwby professed that the type of bonding a child has with his or her primary caregiver will serve as a model for how that child will forge adult relationships. The three main types of adult attachments are secure (70 %), anxious-avoidant (20 %), and anxious-ambivalent (10 %) (Pervin & John, 2001). This work is not a clinical investigation on attachment personalities so no assessment of any kind is made. The general importance here is simply on how being emotionally "attached" to a legal case may help foster parasocial interaction and court case involvement.

One way that news stations promote viewer attachment is by making newscasters attractive and consistent in their presentation style and demeanor (A. M. Rubin et al. (1985). Some basic strategies to cultivate spectator attachment to a media court case is for media personalities to coax viewer investment by speaking directly to the camera, engage in self-disclosure, and request viewer feedback (McCourt & Fitzpatrick, 2001). It appears that getting the viewer more actively involved in the unfolding drama aids in strengthening viewer attachment, and thus PSI. Tru TV is well known for using this tactic in covering legal cases. They encourage viewer involvement and attachment to any particular case by holding quizzes and polls. Two common involving devices are called "the 13th juror" (where viewers give opinions on the case as it unfolds) and "courtside quiz" (where viewers pick right answers on facts about a case). This tactic is solely intended to increase viewer attachment to a case, which Tru TV knows will entice them to want to keep following the case.

Cole and Leets (1999) in a study on TV viewer's parasocial relationships found that adult attachment models can be applied to attachment styles to media. They believe that PSI is influenced by the same psychological mechanisms that shape real social relationships, and that such PSI relationships activate attachment feelings and thoughts that fulfill some attachment needs. Kirkpatrick (1994) concluded that adult attachment style (secure, avoidant, ambivalent) significantly impacts imaginary relationships with television characters. It has been found that anxious-ambivalent types are the most likely to form a parasocial relationship with media personalities, while those that are anxious-avoidant are the least likely to form parasocial bonds (Cole & Leets, 1999).

Tsao (1996) found that parasocial relationships were more of an extension for those that already have strong social relationships and was not solely for the socially inept. Turner (1993) found a positive correlation between PSI and one's self-esteem, suggesting that PSI and real social interaction are complimentary. Stated differently, those with a secure attachment style and good social skills are just as apt to form a parasocial relationship with a media personality as anybody else, especially if the persona is perceived as attractive (Boon & Lomore, 2001). Cohen (2004) found that secure viewers (who are most likely to have satisfying relationships) are just as likely to form parasocial relationships as avoidant types (who are most likely *not* to have satisfying relationships), thus suggesting that PSI should be viewed as an extension of viewer's social relationships, not as compensation for the lack thereof. Understanding the role of viewer attachment to media persona will assist in comprehending the overall portrait.

Chapter 5
The Fun is Escaping

Escapism

The daily routines for many individuals in modern society may leave them longing for change or some excitement in their lives. Dropping the kids off at school, going to the store, eating dinner, and then going to bed at night to prepare to do it all over again often leaves the individual feeling under stimulated and bored with life. Evolutionary psychologists and sociobiologists would argue that humans have an inner drive to explore new places and try new things. The repetitive schedules of most adults in American society stifles these needs and causes pent-up energies. The drive to reduce the mundane and often boring activities of everyday life may motivate individuals to seek an outlet.

Jacklyne, a 22 year old college student:

The general public does not get the whole story what went on so what we do get is a glimpse of something that is entertaining to watch or read. I have one friend that constantly watches celebrity court cases. I believe she watches the cases because her life is not exciting enough so she resorts to watching and following the cases. She probably in some way wants to be a celebrity and live that lifestyle which is much different from her own. There are probably psychological factors that are complex that go into watching the life of a celebrity. Since our culture has accepted celebrities as being these amazing people it is alright to become fixated on their every move. Then you hear about the occasional stalker of a celebrity and wonder how things got so out of control to start stalking someone. That is really what the paparazzi do for a living.

Rick, a 39 year old registered nurse:

I watch famous people on television and in these court trials because they are attractive. I couldn't really care less about the male celebrities but I love looking at those hot Hollywood chicks. It takes you into a fantasy world where you get to imagine living that exciting life and having everything. You always wonder what it would be like to have all that money and fame.

Enter the media.

Figure 2. Illustration of escapism.

    Humans have a strong need for fantasy and often perceive the world through imagination. One of the most common ways that people fulfill their fantasies is through escaping with media. The first intellectual to write about the notion of *escapism* was Montaigne. He set forth the idea that people must escape from reality to preserve their mental welfare (Vorderer & Knobloch, 2000). Media theorists of escapism largely believe that for most people life is unsatisfactory and that most people are limited in their abilities to rearrange their circumstances and are thus left longing for a emotional sedative (Zillman, 2000a). The media thus acts like a sedative by distracting people from ruminating on their boredom (Katz & Foulkes, 1962; Lowenthal, 1961). Escapism can be thought of as a sort of avoidance of reality. Vorderer and Groben (1992) posited that media usage is an effective way to forget about the shortcomings of everyday life. They go on to say that media escapism fulfills both psychological and social functions for the media user.

    But what exactly do people do with the media? How is the media used to escape? Some theorists have argued that the socially depraved use the media to enter a dreamlike world to meet psychological gratifications lacking in their real lives (Morgan, 1984; Perloff, Quarles, & Drutz, 1983). Here it is believed that high exposure to mass media content helps to alleviate tension and satisfy psychological drives by allowing the viewer vicarious participation in the lives and adventures of media characters. In other words, these types of media users seek psychological refuge in the mass media and its various contents. Katz and Foulkes (1962) said that many theorists of escapism seem to view it as "a kind of checking of one's social roles at the movie-house door...(it) seems to mean identifying with a star or hero to the point that one loses oneself in a dream..." (p. 384). For these theorists escapism is a way of deflecting the pain of boredom or social inadequacies.

Other theorists of escapism argue that it is not a tool solely for the psychologically unsatisfied. A. M. Rubin (1981, 1983, 1984) suggested that media escapism is a normal response to television viewing and has little or nothing to do with being socially inept. His studies show that normally functioning, mentally healthy individuals like to "escape reality" sometimes and will often use the media to fulfill these fantasies. From this perspective escapism is not dysfunctional but is a normal response to the human need for fantasy and psychological gratifications (Cacioppo & Petty, 1982; Katz & Foulkes, 1962).

Jackueline, a 33 year old health administrator:

> Celebrity court cases are often sensational and absurd. They make for interesting cases and good entertainment. Ultimately they are cases involving people we all feel like we know on some level, so it stands to reason that we would have a vested interest in watching the outcome of the trial. In the cases of Lindsay, Britney, Nicole, and Paris, I believe that women, especially, get off on watching these girls with perfect lives ruin everything for themselves. It gives the watcher gratification to see the beautiful people crash and burn. It's a quick and cheap ride to a moral high ground.

Valkenburg and Peter (2006) identify two versions of escapism. They believe that people engage the media primarily because of an overproduction of unpleasant fantasies that leads to either "thought-blocking" or "boredom-avoidance." Individuals that are actively thought-blocking are believed to delve into media fantasies in order to drive away unpleasant thoughts and affects. Individuals engaged in thought-blocking are attempting to wash away unpleasant, mundane fantasies with more exciting ones. McIlwraith (1998) said that those with an unpleasant fantasy style frequently watch television in an attempt to escape their thoughts. Thought-blockers are believed to use the media primarily to escape negative or unpleasant thoughts and emotions. They do this by allowing the narratives and/or imagery in the media to preoccupy their cognitions and to push unwanted thoughts and feelings far enough back to where they are out of conscious awareness.

The second version of Valkenburg and Peter's (2006) escapist hypothesis is that of boredom-avoidance mentioned previously. Here the media user is engaging the mass media not to escape unwanted thoughts or feelings but to escape boredom and lack of affect. Boredom-avoidance prone individuals have "poor attentional control" and especially like fast-paced media entertainment to stimulate fantasy. Valkenburg and Peter (2006) posited that a primary function for the boredom-avoidant viewer in watching large amounts of television is to control mind wandering and drifting thoughts. Apparently, then, becoming consumed in an action plot helps to focus the wandering mind on a single event and helps to regulate uncontrollable drifting thoughts. Stated differently, the bored-avoidant prone can ease cognitive drift by becoming engaged in and preoccupied with an entertaining program.

This study will focus on the concept of escapism in terms of how media spectators allow themselves to "escape" in the drama of an unfolding high-profile celebrity court case. Although there has currently never been a study conducted on this concept in relation to watching court cases there is no discernable reason to expect that the psychological needs and gratifications satisfied are any different than when one escapes into a typical television program. As discussed earlier in this work, celebrity court cases involve all of the action, drama, and suspense found in Hollywood movies or television programs (sometimes even more...) and should serve the same basic psychological needs and motivations. There is no reason to believe that these engaging court cases are not also prime grounds for fulfilling viewer fantasy, regulating unwanted thoughts, and alleviating boredom in the same ways that ordinary television programs do. It is being argued here that psychological escapism serves the same basic functions regardless of the medium employed (e.g., TV, Internet, movies) or the content being taken in by the media user (e.g., science fiction, action, soap opera, celebrity court case).

Henning and Vorderer (2001), two leading researchers in the area of escapism, believed that one's "need for cognition" heavily influences whether or not one likes to escape into television programs. Need for cognition refers to "a need to structure relevant situations in meaningful, integrated ways...it is a need to understand and make reasonable the experiential world" (A. R. Cohen, Stotland, & Wolfe, 1955, p. 291). The need for cognition can be thought of as the tendency for some people to actually "enjoy" thinking. What Henning and Vorderer (2001) found is that people low in need for cognition are more strongly drawn toward media viewing than those who are high in need for cognition. What they are suggesting is that people who like to get lost in their own thoughts (high need for cognition) do not like to be distracted by media content as much as people who are attracted to its distracting effects (low need for cognition). They do not suggests that both "types" either like or dislike media, they are simply pointing out that people who like external mental distractions are more likely to find escape in media content; especially television.

Henning and Vorderer (2001) also break escapism down into three interesting branches. The first branch is *social-psychological escapism* which concerns the immediate social setting of the individual and serves as compensation for lack of satisfying social interactions. The second branch is *sociological escapism* which holds that people escape in media because of an overall feeling of being disconnected from the larger society. This entails feelings of isolation, alienation, and anomie. The third branch of escapism is *individual-psychological escapism* which pertains to various aspects of the personality unaffected by social interactions and social settings. This present study in celebrity court cases will touch on the different levels of escapism but will not make an issue out of which type any particular viewer is following. Restated, for the purposes of the current project escapism will be treated more or less as a single-tiered construct and will take the position that viewer escapism is simply "viewer escapism" and makes no attempts to further distinguish between levels.

If a primary motive of escapism is to get away then one must ask, "Get away from what?" Vorderer (1996) believed it is to get away from current social and psychological situations that place too much pressure and demands on the individual. Negative feelings and demands of reality may push the individual to "leave" reality and get lost in media exposure. Kubey (1986) proposed three basic reasons people like to escape in television programs: a) Negative experiences at work cause gravitation toward television escapism at home, b) Negative experiences in social interaction with others will encourage heavier viewing and escapism, and c) Individuals finding themselves in "non-activities" (e.g., staring out a window, waiting, daydreaming) are more likely to find escape in television. The main thing to understand about media escapism is that it is a means for the individual to get away from some aspect of reality. This motive could stem from several factors such as social isolation, lack of satisfying relationships, boredom, negative feelings, demands of life, need for cognition, psychological insecurities, and stress. The point is that, for whatever reason, many people like to "leave" reality, at least temporarily, and escape into the world of television and other forms of media.

Celebrity court cases should prove to be a prime arena for psychological escapism. The viewer can "get lost" in the action. The unfolding drama, the key players, and the conflict, all combine to give the spectator fertile ground to escape in. The fantasy of going through what the celebrity is going through, the intense social interaction, and the exciting psychological atmosphere in the courtroom should prove to be very appealing to one looking for a mental escape from their reality.

Taban, a 41 year old property investor:

> *[I watch celebrity court cases] to escape, because it's just a way to escape everyday life and to see what's happening in other people's lives....The fact that we consider celebrities to be the movers and shakers of our society today and are so addicted to them makes us believe that what happens in their lives is so essential to ourselves that we must keep attention to it. It is just like having an immediate family member who is taking part in a court case. Our analogy is that we face [sic] specific importance on specific people (and in this case celebrities) but reconsider [sic] their welfare and immediate well being important to us.*

Alienation and Escapism

Another psychological variable that should be linked with heavier media usage, particularly television, is viewer *alienation*. Whenever a person feels disconnected from others they may experience a lack of physiologic arousal and thus seek fulfillment in the media. Bardo and Mueller (1991) and Aluja-Fabregat (2000) stated that a sense of alienation may lead to sensation seeking which often times is satisfied in media use. In studying adolescent alienation, Oetting and Donnermeyer (1998) viewed this construct as meaning the lack of functional ties with school, family, and friends. They believe that when a teenager or young adult lacks real connections with primary socializing agents they are likely to experience psychological alienation thus leading to heavier use of media.

Alienation can be conceived of as social isolation. Although one may be in close physical proximity of others this does not mean that he or she is psychically connected to them in any way. A person can be surrounded by other people all day and still feel disconnected and emotionally distant. Alienation can also be thought of as feeling anomic. Emile Durkheim (1893/1933; 1897/1951) conceived of *anomie* as being a state where there is little or no social control of member's behaviors thus leaving them feeling "out of touch" and alone. Feeling anomic is feeling alone and separated from others. Having this sense of anomie can cause one to feel psychologically isolated and propel them to seek a "connection" by escaping in the media. If viewers can form parasocial relationships with media personalities then it should make sense that those feeling alienated may try to calm this psychologic discomfort by seeking escape in the media.

Alienation can be thought of as a psychological or sociological variable. Psychological alienation may be conceived of as an emotional withdrawal from others. This is when the individual closes down and shuts himself off from others. An example of this could be the father that comes home from work, sits down in front of the television to escape from reality, and all the while refuses to connect with his family by holding in his feelings and emotions. He is physically there, but psychologically he is alienating himself from others. Sociological alienation is where the individual is literally separated from others. He may find himself spending most of his days alone and isolated from others. This does not mean he does not actually see or speak to anyone else throughout the entire day, it just means that a large portion of his life is spent pretty much alone and physically alienated from other people. Humans are social beings, and this sociological alienation should be expected to have detrimental effects on his well-being. Some examples would include the coal miner who is buried deep within a mountain all day, an isolated crew on an oil tanker, the solitary academic (who often write about how alienating scholarly writing is and the stress it puts on one's private life), and the socially awkward who literally have no close friends or social networks. For the purposes of this work psychological and sociological alienation will be treated as one and the same. Alienation will be viewed as a sense of isolation and aloneness regardless of whether it is physical, mental, or both.

One may escape in media if one is feeling alienated from others or alienated from the self. If a person is experiencing periods of negative affect during idle times that that person may experience a sense of alienation from self and turn to unstructured activities such as television viewing (Morgan, 1984; A. M. Rubin, 1983, 1985). Kubey (1986) explained the association between viewing amount and negative affect during idle periods and unstructured activities by penning:

> Individual's experience of alienation from self translates into negative experiences during idle time because it is during such time that people necessarily come into greater contact with the self. For those most alienated from [the] self, television offers a ready means of structuring attention that permits both escape from and avoidance of the discomfort that normally occurs during idle time. (pp. 116-117)

This escape from idle time stems from feeling alienated and should promote television viewing which is heavily structured. Shows come on at certain times and air on certain channels on certain days. The shows are rigorously thought-out where the speech, manner, and style of the media persona are heavily orchestrated.

38

For the most part, court cases are heavily structured. The judge sits in front and faces all others, and he or she is in charge of the proceedings. The lawyers sit at their designated tables and must follow the procedural rules of the court. The jury sits in the box and (hopefully) listens intently to the facts and testimony, etc., etc. There is patterned structure in courtroom proceedings and this may allow a person experiencing negative affect due to idle time and discomfort with self a means of escape. If a person is experiencing a sense of alienation then a high-profile celebrity court case just may be the remedy. It offers the alienated individual the opportunity to escape into the unfolding drama, enter the lives of the key players, engage in the disputed conflict, and "connect" with others in a parasocial way. Alienation is an important variable to keep in mind when trying to understand (in its totality) why so many people follow celebrity court cases.

Chapter 6
Lonely Days and Lonely Nights

Loneliness

Another important psychological variable to discuss when attempting to understand why people use the media is *loneliness*. Perlman and Peplau (1981) defind loneliness as "the unpleasant experience that occurs when a person's network of social relations is deficient in some important way" (p. 31). Loneliness has been shown to be correlated to several personality characteristics including shyness, feelings of alienation, low self-esteem, belief that the world is not a just place, and external locus of control (Jones, Freemna, & Goswick, 1981; Russell, Peplau, & Cutrona, 1980). Lonely individuals appear to have more restricted social activities and fewer relationships than non-lonely people (Peplau, Russell, & Heim, 1978).

Raquel, a 25 year old Spanish actress:

Sometimes I feel depressed and want to connect more with celebrities, I think I feel their pain or that I could even give them good advice in their life's [sic] just because I went through the same experience... I believe that human beings are the same all around the world. So, I do believe that the rest of people like to watch celebrities struggle, for the very same reason that I do...loneliness, and the personal situation I'm living right now.

Eric, a 41 year old Internet researcher:

We just live in a society where everybody is isolated all the time. Is it any wonder that people would turn to the media for some sort of relief from the boredom and redundant lifestyles that most people have. You get up in the morning, work all day, work all night, and even work on the weekends. Life sucks.

40

Figure 3. Illustration of loneliness and how the media can serve the function of keeping company with someone that is alone.

Relationships are the core of human social life. Humans are social creatures, and people who do not have real connections with others are likely to feel lonely. Perloff et al. (1983) believe that loneliness is largely a result of social isolation. They say the socially isolated usually have more time on their hands and fewer entertainment options that the non-isolated and will turn to television because it "provides psychological compensation for the loneliness that may result from being alone too much" (p. 352). For this team of researchers loneliness can be attributed to several situational variables. One variable is "dissatisfaction with relationships" where a person is lacking connectedness with others and will turn to mass media for companionship and other psychological gratifications. The assumption is that relationship dissatisfaction (e.g., dating, friends) causes media use rather than the other way around. A second variable is age, which the team believes holds strongest for adolescents, college students, and the elderly, who will often turn to media (especially television) to alleviate feelings of loneliness. They further ague that adolescents and young adults tend to be especially lonely and dissatisfied. Another important variable Perloff et al. (1983) focus on is depression. They found that depressed individuals, who often feel lonely, turn to television to escape their negative affect and loneliness.

Prior research suggests that loneliness is essentially an internal psychological state. Additional variables that correlate with being lonely include feelings of emptiness, awkwardness, boredom, social inhibitions (e.g., making friends), anxiety, and feelings of being unattractive (Goswick & Jones, 1981; Horowitz & French, 1979; Loucks, 1980;

Perse & A. M. Rubin, 1990). Lewis, Dyer, and Moran (1995) saw loneliness stemming from deficient social relationships with peers, family, or friends. They say that lack of interpersonal communication is one of the primary underlying dimensions that may cause an individual to feel isolated and lonely. Kim, Kim, and Kang (2003) believed that a common way people try to alleviate loneliness is through means such as entertainment and socializing. A dominant form of entertainment is mass media usage.

McWhirter (1997) noted that loneliness is a highly subjective experience that can be broken down into "intimate loneliness" and "social loneliness." What is meant by this is that certain individuals may have many friends and still feel lonely, while another individual may have relatively few friends and not feel lonely at all. So it appears that some studies have found loneliness is not simply a result of social isolation but is largely contingent upon the individual's perception of his or her achieved level of social interaction and his or her desired level of social interaction.

If loneliness truly is an internal psychological state then "loneliness" must exist on an individualized continuum. A. M. Rubin et al. (1985) supported this notion by their investigation of loneliness as being conceptualized as the discrepancy between the social interaction an individual needs and the amount of social interaction that he or she feels in being fulfilled. In holding with the position that loneliness is largely a subjective experience, Sermat (1978) penned in a popular study that loneliness is "an experienced discrepancy between the kinds of interpersonal relationships the individual perceives himself as having at the time, and the kinds of relationships he would like to have, whether in terms of his past experience or some ideal state that he has actually never experienced" (p. 274). These interpersonal relationships needs have been formed by individual and social characteristics that lead to motives for need fulfillment and satisfaction (Rosengren & Windahl, 1972; A. M. Rubin et al. 1985).

It has been estimated that 10 to 30% of people have experienced loneliness for a large portion of their lives (Sermat, 1980); but this experience is not solely due to social isolation. It is the cognitive appraisal one gives to her quality or quantity of social contact that is the deciding factor (Peplau, Russell, & Heim, 1979). Perse and A. M. Rubin (1990) pointed out two reactions to this cognitive appraisal: First, some people are driven to reduce (or eliminate) loneliness by finding things to do or initiating social interaction, and second, some people will fall down the path of hopelessness, boredom, passivity, and depression. As will be pointed out later, many people will take the former route and turn to media to alleviate their feelings of loneliness.

If as many as 25% of American adolescents and adults will feel excessively lonely over any 2-week period of time (Z. Rubin, 1979) then it makes sense that many will turn to the media for relief. Schultz and Moore (1984) found that 37% of people watch television or listen to music to lessen feelings of loneliness. Additional studies have found that between 34 and 61% of participants watch television as a common response to loneliness (Rook & Peplau, 1982; Rubinstein & Shaver, 1982). Other studies have found no direct correlation between loneliness and media usage (Austin, 1985); chronic loneliness, media usage, and psychological gratification (Perse & A. M. Rubin, 1990); or severe loneliness, media use, and improved social relations (Finn & Gorr, 1988).

Anthony, a 23 year old student:

> *I think many people in this world are very lonely or sometimes depressed and watching these cases will give them hope and satisfaction. Even the most famous and wealthiest people are suffering....I have a female cousin who graduated a year ago [college] and is currently jobless. She is overweight and is addicted to television and magazines. She is very a very depressed person due to the fact that she is in love with a guy who shows her no interest. She spends her whole day watching television and is addicted to these cases [celebrity]. I personally believe that these cases help her with her depression as she realizes that she isn't the only one going through hardships in life...She knows everything about every single celebrity court case.*

One explanation for the discrepancy in research findings may be due to the way the phenomenon of loneliness has been treated. Mikulincer and Segal (1990) argued that loneliness is a qualitatively complex variable and should be studied from an attributional perspective. According to Canary and Spitzberg (1993) there are two attributionally distinct forms of loneliness. *Situational loneliness* is a short-term affect due to changes in life's circumstances (e.g., relational breakup, loss of job). Individuals suffering from this type of loneliness usually overcome it fairly quickly and do not develop dysfunctional social attitudes and behaviors. *Chronic loneliness* is a long-term feeling of deprivation. Individuals suffering from this are prone to becoming socially incompetent, solitary, unhappy, dysfunctional behaviorally and attitudinally, depressed, uninvolved, and socially isolated (Bell, 1985; Bell & Daly, 1985; Canary & Spitzberg, 1993; Snodgrass, 1989; Spitzberg & Canary, 1985; Spitzberg & Hurt, 1989). Finn and Gorr (1988) found that chronically lonely people use the media as much as situationally lonely people but do not receive the same level of gratification from it. Perse and A. M. Rubin (1990) and A. M. Rubin (1984) suggested that as loneliness persists, viewer satisfaction diminishes because people become less instrumental users of media, more habituated, more apathetic, and less trustworthy of content (e.g., news stories).

If human beings have needs, and these needs are not being met, then a person may turn to an alternative activity for satisfactions. Enter the media. It has been argued in many studies that people frequently turn to media to alleviate or distract them from situational and chronic loneliness (e.g., Austin, 1985; Canary & Spitzberg, 1993; Donohew, Palmgreen, & Rayburn, 1987; Ferle, Edwards, & Lee, 2000; Finn & Gorr, 1988; Perse & A. M. Rubin, 1990; A. M. Rubin et al. 1985). For example, Perse and A. M. Rubin (1990) reported that lonely people watch television as a compliment, supplement, or substitute for real interaction with family, friends, or other social activities. They also report that loneliness increases withdrawal, passivity, and boredom, which further increases use of mass media (especially television). As can be seen time and time again, television proves to be the number one choice of media usage for most Americans; this is why it comes up most frequently in the relevant literature and will be the most referenced in this current study.

Media are often used by lonely people as a functional alternative to actual social interaction. Because many lonely people are unsuccessful at establishing satisfactory relationships with others (not because of a lack of motivation, but because of a dysfunctional psychological state) they often will try to meet their needs through media use (A. M. Rubin & R. B. Rubin, 1985). It is believed that such behavior is purposive, goal directed, active, and intentional (A. M. Rubin et al. 1985). It has been disseminated that a large number of teenagers watch television at home usually to fill time, kill boredom, reduce loneliness, dispel negative affect, and cope with life's pressures (Kurdek, 1987; Ferle et al. 2000). Kim et al. (2003) conclude that teenagers will frequently turn to heavier use of media (e.g., magazines, radio, television) the more lonely they feel. In essence they say that increasing amounts of intimate and social loneliness will lead to increasing amounts of media usage. This speculation appears to hold for adults as well (in Perse & A. M. Rubin, 1990; A. M. Rubin et al. 1985).

Negative social experiences will often lead the individual to substitute television for social activity (Kubey, 1986). When social needs or intimate desires cannot be met in actual relationships people will frequently turn to the media for gratification (Katz, Gurevitch, & Haas, 1973; Rosengren & Windahl, 1972). Although some studies did not find television to be a purposefully employed medium for overcoming chronic feelings of loneliness (Finn & Gorr, 1988; Rubenstein & Shaver, 1982) many have found it to be used for such (as cited earlier), so as it will be treated in the current project. It will not be of interest here as to why people do *not* watch celebrity court cases to alleviate or distract them from feelings of loneliness. The interest is in why they might, have, or *do* watch celebrity court cases to lighten this negative affect.

There has not yet been a study on loneliness and watching or reading about high-profile court cases but there is no reason to think it would be significantly different than the studies that have been done on this psychological variable and news consumption. Several studies have shown that lonely individuals will often turn to news programs to feel "connected" to the outside world and also to lighten their emotional state (Perse & A. M. Rubin, 1990; A. M. Rubin, 1984; A. M. Rubin et al. 1985; A. M. Rubin & Perse, 1987). The common finding is that the lonely will more often rely on news content to satisfy, in part, social needs. Celebrity court cases should also serve to meet these needs. The lonely can stay connected to the outside world through following an intensively covered trial. The celebrity, the key players, and the unfolding drama may all aid in alleviating the viewer's lonely state.

Chapter 7
Divert Your Attention!!

Diversion

Different people engage the various forms of media for different reasons. Regardless of what any particular individual's goals are everyone reads or views media with a purpose. This "purpose" is essentially fueled by the needs and motives unique to each person. The media are so popular because they satisfy, on some level, the spectator's social and psychological interests. Katz, Blumler, and Gurevitch (1974) explained this process:

> The social and psychological origins of needs, which generate expectations of the mass media or other sources, which lead to differential patterns of media exposure (or engagement in other activities), resulting in need gratifications and other consequences, perhaps mostly unintended ones. (p. 20)

The media basically serve to fulfill the viewer's needs. The media can be considered as "agents of diversion and entertainment" that connects the individual's needs and goals to "outcomes of media use" with preferences linked with motivation, selectivity, dispositions, and viewing activity (Katz, Gurevitch, Haas, 1973; Klapper, 1963; A. M. Rubin, Haridakis, Eyal, 2003).

Viewing motivation has been widely studied (e.g., Greenberg & Woods, 1999; Kim & Ross, 2006; A. M. Rubin, 1983, 1985; Watkins, 1988). In these projects the basic principle is that people fundamentally know why they view certain media forms and content and the gratifications they receive from it. A central motivation that viewers have in regard to delving into media content is to pass time or forget about negative thoughts and feelings. This "passing of time" is known as *diversion*. Some of the primary motives of diversion are to "kill time," put off life's tasks, seek enjoyment, relax, and alleviate boredom (A. M. Rubin, 1981, 1985). Kim and Ross (2006) found that one of the main reasons the video game market is approaching sales of $50 billion is because players can engage the action for hours on end and divert themselves from things such as boredom and having to face life's responsibilities.

Jessica, a 30 year old social worker:

> *Diversion is a major reason for my watching celebrity court cases because sometimes I don't want to do what I know I need to do. I need some me time and turning on the T.V. at times seems the easiest thing to do. Sometimes I can get too distracted and really have to pull myself away from the tube. This is why I don't have a T.V. in my room.*

A preeminent scholar in the area of mass media and viewer needs and motivations is Alan Rubin. He conceived of diversion as being a habitual act where the individual utilizes media because "it's something to do" and "passes the time away" (A. M. Rubin, 1976, 1979, 1983, 1985, 2002). Rubin saw media use as "active" where individuals are driven by their needs for gratification (A. M. Rubin, 1981). He has focused a large portion of his academic career on investigating the links between television usage and viewer motivations. He has consistently found strong correlations between the motive to pass time and watching comedy shows, soap operas, action shows, sports, drama, talk shows, and game shows (e.g., 1981, 1983, 1985, Rubin et al. 2003). In fact, in comparing his eight motivations, passing time was the second highest at $r = .38$, second only to arousal at $r = .40$ (1981). This same study yielded interesting negative correlations between viewing to pass time and talk-interview shows and news programs ($r = -.11$, $r = -.19$, respectively). He said that the main reason for this is that "pass time" viewers tend to be younger, prefer comedies, and do not watch news and talk programming.

This negative correlation between young viewers and celebrity court cases is not a concern here because it is generally known that the viewers of news programs and other genres that cover political, economic, or criminal issues of the day are more mature adults, not children or adolescents. In another study A. M. Rubin (1985) opined that television genre is not a relevant point because ritualized viewing can always occur. Here he explained diversion as containing elements of amusement, relaxation, and entertainment. He stated that one of the main motives for viewing any television program has to do with a "more habitual use of television for diversionary reasons" (p. 243) that is fundamentally about filling time. Other researchers have also found diversion to be a main reason for watching television (e.g., Compesi, 1980; Greenberg & Woods, 1999; Perse & A. M. Rubin, 1988; Woods, 1998).

Jackie, a 21 year old college student:

[I watch celebrity court cases] because I want to kill time or put off homework.

Television is the most studied and utilized from of media for psychological diversion (Finn & Gorr, 1988; Lull, 1980; McGuire, 1974). If an individual is stressed about something in his or her life, feels external pressures, or is simply bored, then he or she will more likely than not look for a course of action that will divert their thoughts and feelings to a more pleasurable state. Television appears to be a good source for fulfilling this diversionary need. If a person is bored that person is facing a stimulus deficit. Television not only aids in satisfying social needs of viewers but also "serves the individual's 'stimulus hunger,' satisfying the exploratory drive that makes the individual characteristically curious, seeking after novelty" (McGuire, 1974, pp. 179-180). Thus, media use can serve to divert the viewer away from negative affect and provide a ready-made external stimulus that satisfies (at least temporarily) psychological hungers.

Rebekah, a 37 year old aspiring nurse:

I watch or read about a lot of the celebrity cases because of diversion. When I'm usually online my web page is Yahoo and they keep things in the headline so I click on it to see what's going on. A lot of times they put celebrities & [and] their issues on every channel. It's hard not to look at it. So I watch it because I'd rather be sitting down than doing chores or studying...I tune into these court cases because I'm bored or need a distraction, because I don't feel up to doing what I'm supposed to be doing. Like chores or studying. I [would] rather just take a few minutes to look on the internet at what interesting things celebrities have done. Who got a DUI and if Brittany [Britney] Spears will eventually appear in court.

Figure 4. Illustration of diversion and how the media is often used as a source of distraction or avoidance of chores and other responsibilities.

Finn and Gorr (1988) conceptualize there to be eight viewing motives, in which four are passing time, habit, relaxation, and arousal. These four motives can be conceived of as falling under the category of diversion (Kim et al. 2003; A. M. Rubin,

1985). Blumler (1985) saw two primary viewing motives as passing time and habit (for lack of resources and leisure outlets), in which he waxed that "varieties of social circumstances might engender certain media-related needs." This includes "the need to compensate via media consumption for a relative lack of socially distributed life chances given more abundantly to others" (pp. 43-44). This would include things such as lack of company, boredom, or lack of a satisfying job, which all may motivate the individual to seek psychological diversion in media use. Blumler (1979) referred to these diversionary tactics as *social compensation* where the person employs mass media to compensate for social deprivation and psychological boredom (Zillman, 1985, 1988b).

Boredom is characterized by low levels of arousal which most likely will motivate the person to seek arousing activities. If a person is motivated to seek relaxation and calm they may be experiencing unpleasantly high levels of arousal which in turn may be causing anxiety (Finn & Gorr, 1988). The media can fulfill either one of these motives through diversionary tactics; so media content "not only has the capacity to excite; it can soothe and calm as well" (Zillman, 1985, p. 229). Thus, the media can be used to both pass time (kill boredom) and calm nerves (relaxation). Blumler (1979) said that people want diversion for different reasons and kinds, including "the relief from boredom and constraints of daily routines derived from chat shows, music, comedy, and other forms of light entertainment" (p. 17). This would be in line with the person using diversion to excite low levels of arousal. Blumler (1979) went on to say that diversion also includes "the excitement generated by adventure serials, quizzes, sports, and competitive games, and even the horse-race appeal of following an election campaign" (p. 17). So the mass media is not the *only* source of diversion, it is simply the most widely used in our modern mass-mediated society.

Tony, a 22 year old college student and custodian:

> *As a student taking a full schedule, I have a lot of homework which I hate doing. I try as hard as possible to divert my attention and keep busy in other ways like media....Watching these cases diverts my attention from more important things I am supposed to be doing such as homework or housework. We all to pass time before starting homework but sometimes we end up spending too long and before we know it, we [have] been watching for over two hours.*

Blumler (1979) viewed diversion primarily as a psychological concept. He saw individuals seeking media diversion when they want to relax, want a good laugh or cry, want to get away from everyday worries, want to pass time, do not feel like doing anything else, and/or want to be cheered up. As can be seen, diversion is a means to divert one's thoughts and feelings away from some unwanted state, or as a means to *seek* a desired state. Blumler (1979) also believed that people would often seek diversion in the media as it is seen by the viewer as a thing to turn to when one is alone. Television may function as a "cover" for one knowing one is alone and thus help them, at least temporarily, forget this fact. It is plausible that the viewer may simply be employing the media to help ease their psychological discomfort and negative affect.

In addition to passing time, killing boredom, and trying to relax, media is also utilized to divert one's attention from life's stressors and pressures. When one has tasks to perform that one does not want to do, he or she may turn to media as a source of diversion away from those tasks. Palmgreen and Rayburn (1979) found that one of the main reasons people watch television is to forget about things they do not want to think about. This could include anything from paying bills, to job stress, to troubled relationships. Greenberg and Woods (1999) referred to this type of diversion as *avoidance*, where one attempts to escape from life's pressures and release tension by distracting themselves with media content. This type of avoidance from the realities of life has been thoroughly investigated with soap operas (e.g., Alexander, 1985; Babrow, 1987; Compesi, 1980; Greenberg & D'Alessio, 1985; Olson, 1994; Shim & Paul, 2007). These studies have systematically shown that a large percentage of the viewing audience of soaps are either avoiding their own unsatisfactory relationships, or are simply filling up free time and killing boredom – either way it is a form of diversion in their lives.

Some researchers have found that people who watch soaps are not avoiding or escaping but are simply relaxing (Greenberg, Abelman, & Neuendorf, 1981; A. M. Rubin & R. Rubin, 1982a; R. Rubin & A. M. Rubin, 1982). They found that many "life satisfied" individuals use television as a source of diversion simply for involvement, excitement, and passing time. Although there has been no direct research on diversion and viewing celebrity court cases there is no reason to assume the intentions and gratifications sought would be significantly different. Be it comedy shows, soap operas, action flicks, or news covered court cases, people will often times engage these various genres out of habit or simply to fill time, relax, kill boredom, or avoid chores and other responsibilities.

Jermaine, a 21 year old aspiring NBA player:

I feel the media is a good way to kill time. It also helps in substituting problems that I have in the real world.

Bob, a 29 year old elementary school teacher:

The main reason I watch or pay attention to celebrity news or court cases would be purely for the fact that I would be killing time. I don't become interested and I don't wonder what the next big story would be. I watch television to pass time. I am impartial to what is on it. If the news is on I can watch any broadcaster. I don't follow weekly shows and don't even recognize most of the celebrities names that are mentioned. Usually my girlfriend has to tell me who they are. If there is a court case, there is a little interest on if they get the right sentence.

Tiffany, a 26 year old interior designer:

> *My biggest motivation for watching TV is the enjoyment and diversion. Somehow, I see these two styles with a connection. When I stress out with my project or lack ideas for my floorplan, I will try to turn on [the] TV or internet to "relax." I am trying to think of some new inspiration while I am watching TV, and also I am trying to enjoy the program I am watching to help me calm down & [and] gain a [sic] clear thoughts. My specific goal for turning on media is for entertainment reasons and to kill time. Sometimes, I am just too lazy to go out or hang out with my friend, but media is one entertainment that does not cost money but really helps you to relax & [and] laugh.*

Polin, a 58 year old marital and family therapist:

> *I don't have much to do during the day so I watch [court cases] to pass time.*

Chapter 8
Please, Identify….

Identification

Why is it that audience members seem to get so involved in the proceedings and outcome of a celebrity court case? Do they have something to gain or lose in the matter? Does it have a real and significant impact on their lives? People that follow high-profile legal cases may appear to believe, on some level, that they "know" what the celebrity is going through and strongly empathize with them. It is as if they feel they are actually going through the legal drama themselves even though they do not actually have anything to do with the case. Many spectators will actually get involved in a peripheral way. Think about the hundreds of fans that would line up daily outside the courtroom in Santa Barbara for the Michael Jackson trial just to show their support for him; or the fans that protested the police and media "harassment" concerning the "unfair treatment" NFL star Michael Vick was receiving after he was arrested for dog-fighting. It is a curious phenomenon, but it appears that whenever a celebrity gets into legal trouble people become "extra" involved in the matter; meaning more than they do in a non-celebrity court case.

At the heart of this involvement lies *identification* with the celebrity. Identification is a constructed process in which a fan, or mere spectator, adopts the celebrity's point of view and circumstances and thus develops an empathic involvement in his or her predicament. The argument in this project is that media audiences come to feel, on some level, that they are going through the conflict themselves and have a real quasi-interest in the outcome. Why else do people get so passionate about these cases? Think about the violence that has erupted after some juries have announced verdicts, or how millions of Americans tune in to see if Britney Spears will lose custody of her children, or if Lindsay Lohan will be sentenced to jail. These cases are highly covered in magazines, television, radio, the Internet, etc., and a primary reason is because people are identifying with the lives and plights of these troubled celebrities.

Tamara, a 27 year old school teacher:

> When I turn on the TV or walk through the lines at the store I can't help but want to pick up the newest edition to Time magazine and all those gossip column magazines—they are all fascinating and they so how [sic] draw me into what is going on. The court cases are a different story. I watch TV and read about the trials in the magazines to see what the results [are] and what the outcomes are of some of these cases. For instance, in the custody cases between Britney Spears and Kevin Federline, [they] are interesting to me because I can relate to what those little boys

*are going through. My parents divorced when I was a young girl and it took a toll
on me, like it is on Britney and those boys.*

Identification has not yet been studied in direct relation to court cases but it has
been researched in several related areas. Jose and Brewer (1984) studied how readers
develop a sense of identifying with characters in texts. They found that character
identification exists in differing degrees based on perceived similarity between reader and
the character, sympathy for the character, and suspense developed by outcome valence
(positive or negative). Their findings suggest that whether or not a reader develops a
positive character position is dominated by the belief that he or she is attitudinally and
behaviorally similar to the character. Other studies have found that having physical
characteristics similar to the media celebrity (e.g., gender, looks) is a strong predictor of
identification formation (Caughey, 1985; R. B. Rubin & McHugh, 1987). Kanazawa
(2002) believed that through social and psychological evolution that gender identification
and sexual attraction toward media personae have become the strongest predictors of
viewer involvement and satisfaction in television viewing. Thus, if a person is physically
attracted to a media figure they will tend to become more involved with their legal plight
and form a psychic identification with them.

Sohil, a 33 year old real estate agent:

*I am personally fascinated with watching, listening, or reading about celebrity
court cases because these give me a glimpse of the lives of celebrities. It is like
having the ability to enter their lives and know that even celebrities who are highly
acclaimed by numerous people in the society have their problems too. Court cases
make these celebrities all the more human because most of the time, they are often
looked a like gods and goddesses of the ancient times who are almost perfect....
Hearing the problems that celebrities get from the court cases they have reassures
me that all people have hurdles that they need to overcome. Even the rich and
famous people need to go through the same process that ordinary people like me
undergo. It makes the world equal to the eyes of an ordinary person like me.*

Tyler, an 18 year old martial artist:

*We all want to be famous, including myself. I grew up watching all these famous
famous athletes and actors. I always wanted to be like them. I guess when a famous
person gets into trouble with the law you kind of sympathize with them. It's not
that I can totally relate to them because they are so rich and famous but I still like
to put myself in their shoes and try to experience what they are experiencing. It's
kind of fun I guess to pretend to be famous.*

Figure 5. Illustration of identification and how audience members may empathize or relate to what the celebrity is going through. This may be a prime motive for some individuals to follow these types of court cases.

It is being proposed here that people like to watch celebrity court cases, in part, because of the connection that they feel toward the celebrity. We now live in a *celebrity-centric* culture where people spend a significant portion of their lives watching, reading about, thinking about, and talking about famous media personae. According to Fraser and Brown (2002) people develop psychological bonds with celebrities and in many ways emulate their lives. People will often dress like celebrities and even alter their speech, behavior, and attitudes to better fit the media personalities that they identify with. Freud (1922/1955) viewed the process of identification as an expression of an emotional tie with someone else. Although he did not link this to media personae there is no reason to assume it would work any differently than a face-to-face other. Boorstin (1962) agrees with this assertion by positing that celebrities are role models, and people will alter themselves to better fit their image.

Celebrity identification not only motivates people to follow high-profile cases but also makes it difficult to imagine the celebrity violating moral norms. Brown, Duane, and Fraser (1997) argued that because of celebrity identification it is very difficult (if not impossible) to convict very popular celebrities of horrible offenses. They pointed out the difficulty many people have in believing O. J. Simpson could have committed a gruesome double homicide. This argument could even hold for a less popular media figure. Take the 2007 mistrial of the Phil Spector murder case where the jury was hung even against such overwhelming evidence. This should all come as no surprise in a media-centric society. Cowen (2000) reported that in 1948 a large poll indicated that 37%

of preteens and teens wanted to be a famous entertainer, and by 1986 a similar survey found that 90% of the top 10 people teenagers emulated and looked up to were famous entertainers.

T. B., a 53 year old property investor:

> *We come to the understanding that such celebrity cases, when either won or lost, creates an empathic ability for us. We empathize with such celebrities; either that or we empathize to those areas of society which are damaged by celebrities....And if you were an individual who does not give great importance to the lives of such celebrities and belong to a group of people which do so [do place importance on the lives of celebrities], then you might be considered and labeled as deviant, in which the end result would be [you would be] the outcast in [sic] from the group.*

One of the main reasons people pay attention to many high-profile court cases is due to the seriousness of the situation. In a murder case a celebrity may be facing life in prison and this is cause for many to have a "vested" interest in its outcome. This "interest" stems largely from the identification one has with the celebrity. According to Burke (1969) identification takes place when a person shares the interests of another person or *believes* that he or she shares the interests of another person. Boom and Lomore (2001) believed that identification with celebrities is rooted in a perceived emotional connection or a sense of intimacy. It is this "shared bond" that causes this individual to take an interest in the happenings of the media figure's life.

Caughey (1985) explained identification with celebrities as a function of attachment with and development of self-identity in the individual. He said that celebrities serve as idealized self-images for spectators because they possess qualities or traits the spectator would like to have or develop in themselves. Thus, spectators will often refine or create changes in appearance, values, attitudes, abilities, etc., to more closely model themselves and identify with the celebrity. Once this ingrained identification develops the viewer will almost naturally feel involved on some level in the proceedings and outcomes of the legal cases he or she follows. Tudor (1974) said that this self-identification occurs when there is a strong sense of involvement where the audience member puts himself or herself in the same predicament and persona of the media personality. When someone feels as though they are actually going through the conflict right along with the celebrity then they will instinctively find themselves involved and interested in the proceedings.

One reason people may identify with celebrities is because they represent what people would like to be. Altheide and Snow (1979) believed that most people's everyday lives are somewhat boring when compared to the eccentric lives of media figures and their situations so this is a very appealing place to focus one's energies. Caughey (1984) pointed out that the social worlds of Americans includes more media personae than actual face-to-face contacts and so celebrity identification on such a grand scale should come as no surprise. In a study on television commercials and celebrity endorsement, Alperstein (1991) found that although people will not usually automatically buy a product or deem it useful just because a liked celebrity endorsed it they still feel a bond of intimacy with the celebrity and will pay closer attention to the commercial and take a deeper interest in its message. This is another good indicator as to why people follow celebrity court cases.

Although the viewer is not actually on trial, that fact that a liked (or perhaps disliked) celebrity is facing a court battle they feel a sense of intimacy in the matter.

Identification requires taking on the perspective of another and walking in his or her shoes: By doing this viewer's become more involved in the plot (Livingstone, 1998). Wilson (1993) suggested that identification with media characters is an imaginative process that is evoked when a viewer feels as though they are experiencing the events as the characters experience them. Cohen (2001) proposed that identification has both empathic and cognitive components where the viewer is emotionally affected and takes on the goals and motives of the media personae. In discussing how identification works, Cohen (2006) elucidated:

> Identifying with the character means feeling an affinity toward the character that is so strong that we become absorbed in the text and come to an empathic understanding for the feelings the character experiences, and for his or her motives and goals. We experience what happens to the character as if it happens to us while, momentarily at least, forgetting ourselves as audience members, and this intensifies our viewing experience. (p. 184)

By this logic, when viewers identify with a celebrity going through a legal case they become increasingly empathic and involved in the drama and suspense as the case unfolds and will, on some level, feel as though they are personally going through this experience as well. This could be a big factor in why so many people cheered when O. J. Simpson was acquitted of murder and many others gasped in horror as if the legal system, and the celebrity prosecutors involved, let them down personally. Recall from the earlier discussion that viewers may also "interact" with key players in a high-profile case other than the celebrity, so identification is also likely to occur with the defense lawyers, prosecutors, judges, etc.

As viewers become more involved in a media experience they become *transported* by the text and plot. Gerrig (1993) spelled out transportation as a process of becoming so involved in the story that the spectator is mentally carried into the narrative. This transportation and absorption into the narrative forges a strong emotional connection with the characters and creates empathy toward their goals, interests, and points of view (Green & Brock, 2000). Transportation toward involvement is believed to be a function of attitudinal, demographic, and physical similarity (Hoffner, 1996; Hoffner & Cantor, 1991; Turner, 1993). Prior studies suggest that viewers will most likely be transported by a media plot that contains characters or media personalities that resemble their own personal character traits or traits they wish they had (Cohen, 2003; Tsao, 1996). In fact Cohen and Perse (as cited in Cohen, 2006) found the most significant positive correlation between viewer identification and celebrities to involve homophily and similarity in background, feelings, and attitude ($r = .45$). On the other hand, Turner (1993) found no significant correlation between similarity in physical appearance and identification with a celebrity; and Perse and A. M. Rubin (1990) and Tsao (1996) failed to provide support for the claim that attitude similarity is a strong predictor of viewer identification.

Cohen (2006) believes that one of the biggest problems facing the comprehension of identification with media personae is its "conceptual fuzziness." He argued that the complexity of the phenomenon has lead to many conflicting findings "that are difficult to disentangle into useful generalizations" (p. 193). He said that in regard to the concept of identification a comprehensive theory has not yet been established (Cohen, 2001; Cohen & Perse, 2003); thus, "conceptual clarity is the first order of business" (Cohen, 2006, p. 193) if researchers are to ever fully grasp the psychological processes involved in viewer identification with celebrities and the needs and interests served by this phenomenon.

J. K., a 63 year old family attorney:

> *I think that our culture is so obsessed to [with] the lives of other celebrities because they feel that they can relate to that person and what they are going through. I feel that maybe they feel like they want to see if the people that are celebrities get treated any differently because they are celebrities or not [sic]. They also like to compare the things that happened to them with the things that happen to the celebrities.*

Although identification has never been researched in relation to celebrities involved in court cases it has been studied in several other celebrity oriented formats and arenas such as celebrity worship (Bogart, 1980; McCutcheon, Lange, & Houran, 2002; Morton, 1997); sports celebrities (Basil & Brown, 2004; Rojek, 2006); celebrity spokespersons (Kamins, Brand, Hoeke, & Moe, 1989; Buhr, Simpson, & Pryor, 1987; Misra, 1990); and celebrity endorsements (Friedman & Friedman, 1979; Kahle & Homer 1985; Kamins, 1990). All of these studies have found support for the belief that viewers will more strongly identify themselves with, and get more involved in, any mediated message or plot involving a famous individual. These studies do not seem to differentiate any mediated effects in terms of whether the celebrity is a musician, actor, singer, athlete, etc., and viewer identification. In other words, celebrity is celebrity regardless of the specialized form of entertainment.

An example of this is the emergence of our sports culture. Rojek (2006) found that sports fans become so involved in the lives of celebrity athletes that they often forge an "over-close" identification with the athlete and actually measure their lives in sync with the athlete's life. Basil and Brown (2004) reported that celebrity athletes literally shape the behavior and attitudes of spectators about current social issues. They found that famous athletes are very powerful in shaping public opinion on issues such as child abuse, AIDS, and steroid use when individuals identify with them. Their basic premise is when viewers identify with a celebrity, that celebrity's position on a social issue mediates the long-term effects of the advocated position. These effects can only take place when the phenomenon of celebrity identification occurs.

The point is that we live in a media obsessed culture where celebrities have an effect on the daily lives of the average American. People watch celebrities, listen to celebrities, and identify with celebrities. A major factor in why people like to watch, read, and talk about high-profile court cases is because they identify with the plight of celebrities. They imagine going through the experience themselves, empathize with the key players, and take a vested interest in the proceedings and outcomes. This is the process of identification and its role in motivating viewers to follow high-profile celebrity court cases.

Chapter 9
Here I am...Entertain me!

Enjoyment: Involvement and Entertainment

An additional motivating factor as to why people follow celebrity court cases is simply the enjoyment they get from it. It can be exciting and suspenseful to watch the conflict in the courtroom. The unfolding drama can excite the senses, arouse the nervous system, and make someone feel as though they are a part of something "big," something "alive." When someone is enjoying a high-profile case they are being entertained by it as well, so the two will be used interchangeably for the purposes of this project.

We live in a culture where people want, and seem to need, to be entertained continuously, without interruption. People in a modern society prove daily that they need to have their regular "fix" from media entertainment. The average individual in American culture spends more time in front of the television than practically anything else. Video game addiction has now made its way into psychological therapies as well as the discipline's nomenclature. College students can barely get through a 50 minute classroom lecture without surfing the Internet on their laptops, or using their latest Blackberry-like devices to peruse around for the latest gossip. For whatever reasons, and I am sure that there are many of them, people are fascinating by celebrities, celebrity gossip, and, especially, celebrities that are in trouble with the law. Humans appear to have an innate desire to be entertained and the media is proving to be the most effective in fulfilling this.

Kyle, a 35 year old maritime worker:

If and when I ever watch celebrity trials it is because they are such idiots! They do the stupidest things in the world. They have everything going for them and they still screw it up. I find it entertaining to watch the debacles. These cases are nothing but spectacles for the masses to enjoy. Which I do by the way. I have to admit that I do get some pleasure out of watching the drama along with the foolishness.

Lidya, a 46 year old small business owner:

They [court cases] are fun to watch. They kinda suck you in.

Figure 6. Illustration of audience involvement and entertainment. The enjoyment audience members receive from following celebrity court case may be a prime motive for watching or reading about them.

Several studies have found that enjoyment is a primary motivating factor in why people use the media, particularly television. Some of these studies have focused on television news (Palmgreen, Wenner, & Rayburn, 1980), sports on television (Wenner & Gantz, 1989; Zillman, Bryant, & Sapolsky, 1979), television talk shows (A. M. Rubin, 1981), and general television viewing (A. M. Rubin, 1983; Finn & Gorr, 1988). A. M. Rubin (1981) found that enjoyment was the number one reason that people like to watch television. This study focused on the motivating factors behind watching various program categories such as talk shows, news programs, sports, soap operas, comedies, dramas, game shows, and musicals. When taken together, it was found that people follow these various genres more for entertainment purposes than anything else. Although Rubin (1981) distinguished in his study between entertainment and arousal/excitement no separation will be made here. It will be taken that one of the main reasons people are enjoying a program is because of the emotional affects (i.e., arousal, excitement, fright, mirth) that they receive from the viewing. To lock in the conceptualization, enjoyment encases arousal and excitement.

Daniel, a 22 year old actor:

> *It's entertaining to see how the celebrities I watch in movies or t.v. [TV] shows live their lives. Their ups and downs can make my day better.*

Jessica, a 38 year old health worker:

Enjoyment is the top reason for watching celebrity court cases because I have come to enjoy watching rich and famous individual's drama. I find myself more than anything criticizing what they are doing not because I am any better but because they have more means to get help yet they don't. Makes me feel "normal" and content with what I have. Also thankful @ [at] times. I must admit I feel sad for them having to put their life [lives] on display.

James, a 52 year old counselor:

I am amazed at how people can be so drawn into this celebrity media, which I think is funny. The whole reason why people watch, from my perspective, is for entertainment, & [and] that is primarily why I watch, for entertainment.

Although no study to date has focused exclusively on how celebrity court cases entertain the audiences, Palmgreen et al. (1980) did find that one of the strongest gratifications obtained from viewing network television evening news programs was that of entertainment. These authors did include excitement as part of the entertainment process. They found strong correlations between gratifications sought and gratifications obtained in regard to entertainment ($r = .64$) and excitement ($r = .54$); meaning that these were primary motives for viewing the news and their intentions were satisfied. A. M. Rubin (1983) also found that entertainment was the strongest predictor of viewer motivation with a correlation ($r = .54$) and mean score (3.71) over all other motivating factors (i.e., passing time, relaxation, escape, habit, information, companionship, arousal, social interaction).

Media enjoyment has often been thought of as an affective response to entertainment products like movies, music, or television (Bosshart & Mocconi, 1998) and it is believed to be best understood from a motivational-psychological perspective (Bryant, Roskos-Ewoldson, & Cantor, 2003). Vorderer, Steen, and Chan (2006) stated that entertainment is controlled by the individual; not the other way around. It is the individual that deliberately decides how and when to be entertained. They say, "As a human activity, it includes various physiological, cognitive, affective, and behavioral components. Therefore, entertainment can and should be described and explained by a discipline concerned with human thinking, feeling, and behavior" (p. 4). Enjoying a media narrative has to do with emotions and cognitions. It is believed here that celebrity court cases excite both of these components and can be best understood in terms of audience needs and motives.

Earlier research has identified entertainment as a core component of media use where audience needs are inferred from media motives (Rosengren, 1974; A. M. Rubin, 1981). It is argued that people have a *need* to be entertained, and this need is at the heart of why people are so motivated to use the media. In an examination of the motivations to watch television A. M. Rubin (1981) concluded that not only is the entertainment motive one of the strongest predictors but, unlike many of the other viewing typologies, entertainment viewers are of all age levels, very attached to the medium, enjoy all types of programs, and watch many hours a week. In other words, people of all ages, social classes, backgrounds, and tastes, employ all genres of television on a regular basis to satisfy their need to be entertained.

This "need to be entertained" is commonly conceived of as being an outcome of a purposive use of media content (Conway & A. M. Rubin, 1991). Blumler (1979) viewed these viewer needs and motives as generating an active audience that select media and program content based on expectations of gratifications. It has been premised that the motive to be entertained by media creates an instrumental orientation that entails intentionality, selection, and media involvement (A. M. Rubin, 1983, 1984). Stated differently, people have a need to be entertained which propels them to actively seek out media content that will instrumentally and intentionally satisfy that need. As Katz (1968) said in his study on mass communication, it is not "what the media *do to* people" it is "what people *do with* the media" (p. 88, emphasis in original). People are constantly and actively seeking to be entertained. Audiences will employ the various media to meet their needs and obtain psychological gratifications.

Entertainment has been viewed as an "intrinsically motivated response to certain media products" (Vorderer, Steen, & Chan, 2006, p. 6) where people believe that their behavior is not under the influence of some external force but is competent and autonomous (Ryan, 1982; Ryan & Deci, 2000). This need for autonomy comes from the individual's intrinsic motivation to believe that their media involvement is self-determined (Reeve, 1996). In further explaining the audience's interest in entertainment, Vorderer et al. (2006) said that self-determination suggests:

> That media consumption in general, and the use of entertainment products in particular, provide specific ways to satisfy the fundamental psychological needs proposed. First, exposure to entertainment products is usually an activity that has an end in itself, and thereby qualifies as being intrinsically motivated. It serves all three fundamental needs of competence, autonomy and relatedness, although these needs materialize over a life span, in different cultures, situations, and even personalities. However, entertainment products are suitable to use nearly anywhere and anytime. (p. 7)

This is in line with the proposal that seeking out media content to be entertained is both universal and active. The media do not *use* audiences; the audiences are willingly and autonomously using the media to satisfy entertainment needs.

Zillman (1985) believed that one of the main motivations to seek media entertainment is to kill boredom. He said that individuals with low levels of arousal will selectively expose themselves to specific program content to manage their moods. One popular means of accomplishing this psychological motive is through watching sports on television. Guttman (1986) penned that viewing television sports is functionally equivalent to spectating in the stadium. Rader (1984) said that if one's motive is to relieve boredom, be stimulated, and reduce tension then sports programming may "fit the bill." Bryant and Zillman (1983) saw sport on television as highlighting competition between "hated foes" who engage the viewer as if he or she is actually participating in the conflict. This vicarious participation is what motivates the viewer and heightens enjoyment.

In discussing the affective involvement and enjoyment that spectators receive from watching televised sports, Wenner and Gantz (1989) explained how the glory, competition, and drama in sports creates a unique, unmatched form of media entertainment. They wrote:

> Sports differ from other programs. Most nonsport entertainment programs are prerecorded, scripted stories with actors playing roles. Plot outcomes are rarely in doubt, protagonists tend to survive, and actors "bloodied" in action show no scars off the set. Most televised sport is live and unrehearsed, and "bloodied" athletes carry scars off the field. Athletes' careers hinge on their performances, and outcomes are uncertain, with the "drama" later reported as news. Reality and uncertainty in sports give its viewing a unique flavor. (p. 242)

This uncertain and unrehearsed truth is a large part of what makes watching televised sports so enjoyable. Zillman et al. (1979) theorized that contact or fast-paced sports are the most involving and enjoyable to the audiences because they tend to be breeding grounds for exciting conflict which stimulates affective responses in the spectators.

A parallel will be drawn here between watching sports on television and watching a celebrity court case on television. In line with Wenner and Gantz's (1989) explanation as to why televised sports are unique and motivate involvement, the same holds as to why celebrity cases are also unique and motivate viewer involvement. Celebrity court cases are also unrehearsed and uncertain. The plot is not scripted and there are no "actors" playing roles. The protagonist (if there is one) may win or lose and will carry the "scars" (e.g., go to prison) if he or she has a bad outcome. The "performances" given in the courtroom may make or break the celebrity's career, just like an athlete's performance will make or break his or hers. The drama in and out of the courtroom is also reported as important news. Thus, just as with televised sports, the spectator will cheer for his or her team, and boo and hiss at the opposing team (think O. J. Simpson murder trial). All of this uncertainty, realism, conflict, and suspense serve to intensify the involvement and enjoyment in following high-profile court cases. Just like when millions of Americans watch televised sporting events weekly (Frey, 1983; Rader, 1984), millions of Americans follow celebrity court cases where the primary motive is to be entertained and the gratifications sought are affective involvement and enjoyment.

Daniella, a 25 year old fashion designer:

Enjoyment is the main reason why I watch the media or listen to it. I think it's so entertaining to know about what is going [on] in celebrities lifes [lives] and I'm always tuned in to what is going on. The drama in their lives is entertaining.

Erica, a 21 year old video game marketer:

[Enjoyment found in media].... *because I love to feel happy and to feel good.*

Michelle, a 49 year old housewife:

*I tend to watch these images and pay attention to them because I find these
celebrities problems and drama infested lives exciting to watch. It purely for me
is based on an entertainment aspect. I think for the most part it is just watching
what kinds of things they get themselves into that is so entertaining....My
motivations in watching or reading about these particular events would be because
I feel that it is interesting. I think it is based in American culture to watch and
be involved in these images. It is a huge part of our society.*

Disposition, Involvement, and Enjoyment

Why is it that some celebrity cases are covered on such an unbelievable scale that
one cannot seem to turn toward any medium without hearing or reading about it, while
others, though widely covered, do not nearly reach the same level of popularity? Some
court cases appear to dominate the major outlets in both print and electronic media and
others are pushed to the back sections of magazines and newspapers or are just a blurb on
major network or cable news channels. Why is it that legal cases like the O. J. Simpson
murder trial, the Anna Nicole death case(s), Paris Hilton's legal troubles, and Britney
Spears' frequent legal clamors dominate news programs and print tabloids from CNN to
the National Enquirer, while other celebrity cases like the Phil Spector murder trial or the
Robert Blake murder trial only receive a fraction of the coverage in comparison? It is
proposed here that a major factor that determines how popular a celebrity court will be is
how the public feels about the given media persona. Does the general public like the
person? Is the common sentiment one of indifference? Does the average person seem to
dislike the famous individual? In other words, what makes watching some celebrity court
cases interesting and enjoyable, and others not all that involving?

One conceptual way to explain this phenomenon is through *disposition theory*,
which accounts for the conditions under which media involvement is enjoyable or not.
Disposition theory explains the process through which the audience develops emotional
connections with the personae they hear and see in media. Its two fundamental
propositions are that enjoyment derived from witnessing the success and victory of a
competing party increases with positive sentiments and decreases with negative
sentiments toward that party; and enjoyment derived from witnessing the failure and
defeat of a competing party increases with negative sentiments and decreases with
positive sentiments toward that party (Zillman, Bryant, & Sapolsky, 1989). The theory
focuses on attributions and moral assessments and then projects enjoyment or dejection
on the basis of these formed dispositions (Zillman, 1996). Stated differently, viewers
form likes and dislikes for the people they see in the media and this has a great deal to do
with their level of involvement and enjoyment in the drama.

Dispositional alignments of viewers to various types of entertainment characters has
been studied in the areas of sports (Bryant, Zillman, Raney, 1998; Sapolsky, 1980;
Sargent, Zillman, Weaver, 1998); violence (Sparks & Sparks, 2000; Zuckerman, 1996),
drama (Vorderer & Knobloch, 2000; Zillman, 1996), humor and comedy

(Zillman, 2000b), and the news (Raney, 2004; Zillman, Taylor, & Lewis, 1998). All of these studies found support for the premise that audience disposition is a strong factor in predicting emotional reactions and enjoyment of any given form of entertainment narrative or news story. Zillman (1998) abbreviated the dynamic of dispositional alignments by stating:

> Specifically, a favorable disposition toward friendlike characters is thought to instigate hopes for benefaction and fears of aversive outcomes. Liked characters, in other words, are deemed deserving of good fortunes and undeserving of bad ones. In contrast, an unfavorable disposition toward enemy-like characters is thought to instigate hopes for aversive, punitive outcomes and fears of benefaction. Disliked characters, then, are deemed deserving of bad fortunes and undeserving of good ones. (p. 201)

Media audiences, after forming dispositions and making attributions, want good outcomes for liked media personae and want bad outcomes for disliked media personae. That is, media users' emotional reactions toward media characters mediate affective response and enjoyment (Raney, 2006).

Regardless of the program type, audiences will typically align themselves with the protagonist, for whom they wish a positive outcome, and stand against the antagonist, for whom they wish *not* to have a positive outcome (Raney, 2004). In accordance with disposition theory, readers and viewers will make moral judgments about the characters in movies, television shows, and news programs (Raney & Bryant, 2002). These moral evaluations form the basis of the spectator's emotional reactions to the characters. Rhodes and Hamilton (2006) elaborated:

> Those characters who behave in accord with the audience's moral code will be evaluated positively; those who behave contrary to the audience's moral code will be evaluated negatively. These evaluations then trigger the audience to experience an emotional affiliation toward the characters. Because of these emotional ties, audiences develop expectations for the outcomes of the drama, such that they wish for good things to happen to the characters they like, and for bad things to happen to the characters they dislike. Enjoyment of the program or movie results when the outcomes are as expected. (p. 125)

Basically, involvement and enjoyment in media programs centers on how audiences evaluate and create affiliations with media personae. This media-enjoyment process is highly dependent on what happens to both the liked and disliked characters; and this holds for all genres. Raney (2006) said "the process by which enjoyment is derived through dispositional affiliations and subsequent anticipatory emotions with media characters is quite similar regardless of the media content" (p. 137). These findings form the basis as to why disposition theory is relevant and as to why audiences take an interest in, and enjoyment of, watching any particular celebrity court case.

Polly, a 41 year old retailer:

My motivation for watching television are [is] for enjoyment. Although I use the internet and read magazines my main source of what's going on comes from television. I find watching TV relaxing at times and also very enjoyable. I don't think I am obsessed with celebrities but I do find their lives interesting.

Ruthie, a 44 year old small business owner:

I really do not believe I get anything from it [watching celebrity court cases] other than entertainment. They never pass the good things that stars do and if they do they make them seem very miniscule compared to the bad things they do. Christina Riche [Nicole Richie] is known for driving the wrong way on the freeway yet not too many people know that she donated all her baby shower gifts to needy families. What the media puts out their [there] for us to see are all the bad things the stars do with the purpose of entertaining us. These people have ordinary lives just like the greater population so putting on the news more "ordinary" events would not catch to [too] many peoples eyes [sic] yet giving them some far out news would work to catch their attention. The entertainment we get from the lives of the stars is close enough to watching the movies. The media has to sell the stories and they add a lot of hype to the stories. I would not say that it fulfills anything in my life other than entertainment.

Cynthia, a 21 year old college student:

I think others find celebrity cases interesting…I find them irrelevant to my life.

Tony, a 23 year old aspiring radio personality:

Like very other American, I love and enjoy reading or watching anything the media has to say about certain celebrities.

Raney (2006) highlighted six psychological factors that can be applied to all media formats. The basic principles of disposition theory are: a) disposition-based theories can predict enjoyment and appreciation of media content based on motives and moral reasoning; b) disposition-based theories can predict emotional response to media content based on empathy and cognition; c) disposition-based theories posit that enjoyment of media content fundamentally revolves around the viewer's feelings about characters; d) disposition-based theories posit that dispositional affiliations toward media personae are formed and maintained on a continuum from extreme positive through indifference to extreme negative affect; e) disposition-based theories rely, in part, on the evaluation of conflict outcomes and fairness between characters; f) disposition-based theories acknowledge that individual differences, personal experiences, basal morality, emotional responsiveness, and many other psychological and social-psychological factors play into any particular alignment and affiliation with any particular media character. Disposition theory does a good job at highlighting patterns in audience reactions and alignments, but it cannot account for every specific person in regard to every specific case because some people will like a certain celebrity while others will not; and this is based primarily on Raney's (2006) six fundamental principles of disposition-based theories.

Because dispositions are based on the moral evaluations of a celebrity's actions and intentions, and because people differ in the way they make moral evaluations, dispositions toward celebrities should differ between individual audience members. Another key factor that determines liking or disliking and following or not following a news story is empathy for those involved (Hoffman, 1987; Zillman, 1994, 2000c). Raney (2002) found that empathy was a significant factor in whether or not people sympathize with the victim of a media crime and enjoy the presentation where the crime is avenged. In studies in reality-based crime drama researchers have found that audiences moral judgments tend to revolve around attitudes about punitive punishment and vigilantism, affect, and cognitive variables (Oliver, 1996; Raney, 2005; Raney & Bryant, 2002). Basically, in crime presentations people want the victim(s) to finish with a hoped-for positive outcome and the perpetrator(s) to face a hoped-for negative outcome.

Affective reactions to events in the news are mediated by dispositions toward the recipients of good or bad outcomes. These affective dispositions then convert normative goodness and badness into subjectively good or bad news, which is unique to each viewer (Zillman et al. 1998). In the case of indifference audience members must be supplied with enough information to align themselves accordingly. According to Raney (2004) indifference toward the characters in a dramatic presentation will result in flat affect where the viewers do not care one way or the other. He says that lack of dispositional intensity may cause ambivalent or neutral feelings toward the media personae and their outcomes. Sharkey (1993) believed that indifference toward a story and lack of affective engagement for those involved can be overcome through "character development." Indifference stems from insufficiently developed characters and this can be overcome by constant attention to the story and supplying vast amounts of pertinent information. Examples of this can be seen when the media frame a crime case and literally turn the key players into famous or infamous media folks (e.g., Scott Peterson, Duke Rape Case, Jeffrey Dahmer).

It is being positioned here that with enough information and media attention that the audience members will eventually align themselves with or against celebrities in legal cases and form unique dispositions toward them. The O. J. Simpson trial was so popular largely because almost everyone had formed dispositions toward the defendant, his defense team, the prosecutors, and even the judge. Whether liked or disliked, millions of Americans had aligned themselves and were affectively engaged in the drama. People wanted to see their hoped-for outcome and took a vested interest in it. Whether on one side of the aisle or the other, everyone involved wanted a positive outcome for those they liked and a negative outcome for those they disliked. Lack of information or affective involvement leads to indifference. The Phil Spector murder trial did not receive nearly the same amount of coverage or emotional involvement as the O. J. Simpson murder trial. Why was this? It could best be explained in terms of indifference and failure of audience members to fully align themselves and form dispositions toward Spector (and maybe even the victim, Lana Clarkson). People simply did not really seem to care what happened to him one way or the other. He was not really "liked" or "disliked"; he was sort of a neutral character that fostered ambivalence toward him.

For audiences to care about the outcomes in news stories dispositions toward those involved must be formed (Zillman, 1991, 1996). Once formed the following predictions can be made in regard to news events:

> 1) News revelations of bad fortune for disliked persons or groups foster positive affect in proportion to the degree of disliking. 2) News revelations of bad fortunes for liked persons or groups foster positive affect inversely in proportion to the degree of liking. 3) News revelations of good fortune for disliked persons or groups foster positive affect inversely in proportion to the degree of disliking. 4) News revelations of good fortune for liked persons or groups foster positive affect in proportion to the degree of liking. 5) After inversion of the liking-disliking dichotomy, negative affect follows the same set of predictions. (Zillman et al., 1998, pp. 156-157)

Celebrity court case involvement and enjoyment should follow these five basic predictions. Once dispositions are formed then audience members should be affectively engaged and concerned about the outcomes. If they like a given celebrity or apply positive attributions to his or her motives and intentions then they should wish for a positive outcome for that celebrity. If the audience member dislikes the given celebrity or applies negative attributions to his or her motives and intentions then they will hope for a negative outcome for that celebrity. If the audience member is indifferent, that is, not emotionally involved, and has not formed any dispositions toward the given celebrity then that person most likely will not care about the outcome either way and they will barely, if at all, follow the case. Disposition theory should aid in our understanding as to why some court cases are so widely covered and trigger such emotional involvement, while others, in comparison, barely get a blip on the media radar screen.

Kevin, a 23 year old college student:

> *I can't speak for everyone, but I can defiantly [definitely] speak for myself on why I listen/watch celebrity court cases. I noticed I enjoy the celebrity court cases for entertainment reasons. I love to know what rich and famous people get themselves into. It's sad to say, but people like myself watch these cases for entertainment.*

Chapter 10
"Did You Hear About What Happened to _____"
(fill in the blank)

Social Use: Information, Conversation, and Decisional Utility

Another motivating factor in regard to watching high-profile court cases is the *use* a viewer can receive from it. There are practical reasons behind why someone would want to follow what is going on with a particular celebrity case: They may be able to apply the happenings to their own daily lives, they may work in the legal field, or may have some other profession that pertains to or is concerned with the happenings (e.g., researcher, social commentator, journalist, teacher), etc. The possibilities are endless, but what is known is that millions of Americans follow and talk about these cases on a regular basis. The focus of this factor is on the social dimensions pertaining to why people are motivated to follow celebrity court cases and the social needs that are being met by it. Again, as of this writing the uses and gratifications stemming from watching court cases is relatively nonexistent. An abundance of research has been conducted on other types of media content which will be used as a segue to the ensuing typological model and as for support for the foundations of the arguments made in this work.

One of the first scholars to study the uses of mass media in regard to an "active audience" was Blumler (1979). In this study he argued that audiences are not passive, but are actively engaged in media use and are well aware of what their motivations are. He believed that media consumption is directed by sought gratifications where people are aware of the benefits they will receive from the media communication. Individual motives will be guided by a process of "selectivity" where media behavior reflects one's interests and preferences. This perspective takes the stance that audiences are not being used by the media, but are using the media to meet certain social and psychological needs.

One of Blumler's (1979) primary motives is *cognitive orientation*, where the viewer seeks to find information about his or her society that can be put to practical use. He refers to this "surveillance" of media as a method of keeping tabs on party policies, politicians, and other issues of the day. Fowles (1992) said that approximately one-quarter of American adults watch television news on a typical weekday and digest the facts presented as true. This does not include the percentage of American adults that get their news from other media sources (e.g., newspapers, Internet). The point is that millions of Americans watch or read about current events in the news on a daily basis, and celebrity court cases are often leading stories.

Suzie, a 52 year old home decorator:

I like to be social & learn new things everyday. I love to talk to people, and learn something different from everyone. I like to read books, magazines, & watch TV shows which will do something for me in the future.

Alexa, a 22 year old recruiter:

The world today is so obsessed with the lives of celebrities. You need to follow along in order to talk to one another...I know that as soon as something big happens my phone will start to ring so someone can tell me about it, and if I hear big news first I will call everyone I know.

Figure 7. Illustration of social use and how people use the information they acquire from the media for socializing and talk with others.

Other researchers have also studied media use from an active orientation where the individual wants to apply it to some social setting (e.g., McDaniel, 2003; A. M. Rubin, 1979, 2002). For example, Huston, Wright, Marquis, and Green (1999) found that children use television to find out about appropriate gender behaviors. Greenberg and Woods (1999) declared that one of the primary gratifications that adolescent females receive from watching soap operas and celebrities is learning about appropriate, or desirable, social behaviors. This social learning factor encompasses things like; learning from the mistakes of others, learning how to act in various situations and places, learning what could happen to ones self, learning about the world, and learning how to do new things. In other words, people use the media to learn about themselves, their worlds, and how to behave and function accordingly. Compesi (1980), in a survey with viewers of the soap *All My Children*, concluded that the primary gratification obtained in watching was the social information by the characters and narratives. Greenberg, Neundorf, Buerkel-Rothfuss, and Henderson (1982) published that regular soap viewers watch largely because it acts as a source for learning how to deal with social problems.

Another type of programming content that has been widely studied in terms of social use is televised sports. Viewing sports on television has been shown to be marked by animated conversations, group viewing, cheering, talking and complaining (Bryant & Raney, 2002; Gantz, 1981; Rothenbuhler, 1985, 1986 [as cited in Wenner & Gantz, 1989]; Zillman et al. 1989). Bryant and Zillman (1983) conceived of sports viewing as a means of bringing people together in groups to bond against a "foe" or opponent. Wenner and Gantz (1989) determined from telephone interviews that one of the main motivations of sports fans involves the social aspects of viewing. They found that explicit companionship with family and friends was a significant reason for viewing. What all of these researchers found in terms of sports viewing is that it is largely seen as a *social* occasion by the spectators. Although "killing time" and "relaxing" were also motivating factors, it is primarily the social companionship that most viewers seem to like in regard to watching televised sports (Gantz, 1981; Wenner & Gantz, 1989; Bryant & Zillman, 1983).

Jasmine, a 33 year old real estate agent:

> *Celebrity court cases are a huge part of the media. Everywhere I am, whether I'm getting my nails done, driving to school, at home watching the news, or surfing the net, I am surrounded by the latest gossip of Britney Spears, Paris Hilton, Lindsay Lohan, Angelina Jolie, and so on! I watch celebrity news because if I don't watch it, then I feel like I am out pf the loop. By being informed on the latest case, [it] is as if I am keeping up with the most important news which has occurred in the world. Everybody is watching and talking about celebrities, and if I don't get my feed, then I can't keep up in conversations. My motivation is the people around me.*

Information and Decisional Utility

One of the common motivations for media use is seeking information (Oliver, Kim, & Sanders, 2006; A. M. Rubin, 2002). In a study on radio listening, Mendelsohn (1964) found that getting useful information was one of the most beneficial aspects of tuning in. Listeners could learn about traffic, the weather, politics, and current events, all of which can be utilized in a way that benefits the listener. Berelson (as cited in A. M. Rubin, 1983) penned that the primary use of newspapers is information gathering, social contact, interpretation of public affairs, and usage for daily living. Many other researchers have found that a primary motive for watching television is to gain information (e.g., McQuail, Blumler, & Brown, 1972; Potter, 2004; Robinson & Davis, 1990; Wicks, 2006). Information gathering may be taken to be a central factor as to why people follow celebrity court cases as well. These cases inform viewers about many things in our society, from how our legal system works, on one end, to what the latest celebrity fashions are on the other (think Martha Stewart).

Pioneering "uses and gratifications" researchers Palmgreen and Rayburn (1979) formulated seven viewing gratifications of public television; of which two were, learning about things, and communication utility. Their argument was that one of the most basic gratifications that viewers get from watching television is gaining information about public issues, crime, current events, politics, home improvements, and life in general. In line with the Palmgreen and Rayburn (1979) study, A. M. Rubin (1983) found that information seeking was a top motivating factor in why people watch television. He posits that people watch television to learn about themselves and others, to learn about things that could happen to them, and to learn how to do things they have not done before. The findings of these studies suggest that people do not simply just want information for the sake of having it; they want to actually do something with it.

The basic question here is: What do people then do with media information? McQuail (1994) and Wicks (2006) spelled out the process by stating that people attend to the message content, note the manner of message communication, consider structure and framing technique, take in relevant information, and disregard unimportant, dull, or irrelevant information. This information processing is mitigated by the audience's attitudes, beliefs, predispositions, and needs (Potter, 2004; A. M. Rubin, 2002). In the context of news information audience members will attend to messages that fulfill certain gratifications (Rosengren, Wenner, & Palmgreen, 1985). A. M. Rubin (1981) said that these gratifications from television viewing can teach people about what is going on in the larger society and better equip them to deal with other people, as well as personal and social problems.

When discussing the gratifications sought by television news viewers, Palmgreen et al. (1980) stated that general information seeking is an effort to survey one's environment and stay connected with political information, They found that "keeping up with current issues and events," and monitoring price changes and "things like that" were all significantly correlated ($p < .001$) with gratifications sought and gratifications obtained. Additionally, they investigated viewer's learning about government officials (e.g., surveillance), making decisions about important issues
(e.g., voting), making social comparisons (e.g., class), and monitoring prices (e.g., inflation, gas). A. M. Rubin (1985) referred to this use of media information as *social utility*, where people view to learn about others and relate to others. Audiences want to understand people's lifestyles, modes of thinking, problems, and problem solving. He said that this social utility function aids viewers in becoming oriented to their worlds and assists in social integration. Again, viewers do not seek information for the sake of just knowing about something. Viewers actually want to utilize this information in a practical way that will service a need or help improve their personal lives and social situations.

Some people watch the news to seek information that will manage their moods in a desired direction (Knobloch-Westerwick, 2006). Biswas, Riffe, and Zillman (1994) conducted a study exploring how people select specific news articles to read based on their feeling states. They found that women tend to select positive news stories when they are in both a negative mood state and a positive mood state, while men in negative states tend to be interested in negative news messages. Zillman (1988a) theorized that people tend to seek out information that will converge with existing attitudes, and this may explain the noted differences in gender news selection and feeling states. Most people will avoid news that creates cognitive dissonance (Festinger, 1957), unless this dissonant information can be utilized in a functional manner, such as adaptation or survival (Knobloch-Westerwick, 2006). To put it differently, viewers, male or female, have hedonic motivations to seek out media content that alters their moods toward a desired state.

The information gathered from following a court cases may assist in attaining that desired state. Watching a celebrity get into trouble may create negative feelings in some spectators, but positive feelings in other spectators. According to mood management theory it all depends on the specific individual's desired state. Why would a young girl that likes Britney Spears continue to watch her downward spiral? According to Hastall, Rossmann, and Knobloch (as cited in Knobloch-Westerwick, 2006) people do not avoid news content that depicts one's own problems (e.g., drug use, crime, romance) as Zillman (1988b, 2000d) proposes, but actively pursue it to find guidance (also; Metzger, 2002). This suggests that people may follow high-profile celebrity cases to get information on how to behave, how not to behave, how to deal with problems, etc. Trepte, Zapfe, and Sudhoff (as cited in Knobloch-Westerwick, 2006) supported this claim in a study that showed that adolescents prefer TV talk shows and informational programming that covers their own current problems so they can learn how to better deal with their situations.

This practical employment of media information is known as *decisional utility* (Palmgreen et al. 1980). Decisional utility refers to using media-garnered information as a tool for making choices in one's everyday life. Swanson (1977) spelled out this type of media gratification as a way to find out about issues that are relevant to one's own self and then making informed decisions about what to do. Blumler (1979) saw news information as a means of tracking what government officials are doing and then utilizing this by making important voting decisions based on this information. In a measure of television viewing motivations, A. M. Rubin (1981) found information utility to be the fifth ranked reason why people generally watch television. In terms of watching news programs and talk-interview shows, information utility had the highest partial correlations with viewing motivations of any of the nine clusters ($r = .04$, $r = .15$, respectively). This implies that the main reason people watch news programs and talk-shows is to gather information that they can use in their daily lives.

When being informed about the mistakes (or crimes) that celebrities have made, audiences learn from this and incorporate this information into their knowledge base and act accordingly; of course viewer's subsequent behavior will be guided by their own unique needs and motivations. The point is that people watch for a reason, and that reason is practical. People often base many of their life's decisions on the information disseminated to them in the media, so the act of paying attention itself is active and intentional. Palmgreen et al. (1980) expressed this pragmatic intention by saying that, "Information is attended to by individuals only because they believe it will prove useful for them. In other words, decisional utility represents *specific seeking* of information useful in decisions about personal or public issues" (p. 169). Again, the premise here is that a contributing motivating factor in regard to why people watch celebrity court cases is decisional utility, which refers to soaking in the information disseminated in the media and applying it to some practical use. People often make decisions based on the information heard or read in the media, and information about celebrities in legal trouble seems to rule the day.

Alexa, a 27 year old receptionist:

The reason I watch or read about celebrity court cases is very simple. It is entertaining, makes me feel better about my life and it gives me something to gossip about. When I get to work in the morning one of the first things I do is go to Yahoo and see if there are any new headlines involving the stars. I can't wait to see what kind of trouble they have gotten themselves into over night. I also like the fact that it gives me something to talk about. I couldn't imagine how boring some of my conversations would be if I didn't keep myself knowledgeable about what was going on. When you are with friends most [of the] times you will turn to a conversation about the latest problems in the lives of Hollywood's finest. If I didn't keep up with what was going on then I wouldn't have anything to talk about. It is also a good ice breaker. I guarantee that within a few minutes we are talking like we are old friends [when starting up a conversation with a total stranger].

Jackie, a 24 year old paralegal:

I work for a lawyer and I ask questions in regards to different cases that involve celebrities [for purposes of talk with others]

Talk: Information and Social Fitness

In a postmodern society it would appear that one of the best ways to demonstrate to other people one's social competence is to have current information about the lives of important celebrities. In a culture dominated by media imagery and fabricated narratives, people seem to place a high premium on having the "inside scoop" on famous people's lives that one does not even know personally. This should come as no surprise in a society where vast numbers of people seek immediate gratifications. According to Vorderer (2000) television has become the number source of social information and entertainment, and is the number one choice for leisurely activity. While watching television (or reading magazines, books, or browsing on the Internet) people can gather an enormous warehouse of information about the lives of famous people; and one of the most exciting times to follow a celebrity's life is when he or she is in trouble with the law. This socially important information gives the individual valuable communicative nuggets and demonstrates to others one's "social fitness."

To be considered "fit" in a social sense a person must be current on pop culture trivia and proficient in discourse concerning the lives of famous people. An important factor to consider when conceptualizing the reasons why people watch or read about celebrity court cases is the social dimension: People love to talk to other people (and maybe even to themselves) about celebrities. This category has been given a variety of names such as "anticipated communication" (McLeod & Becker, 1974), "communication utility" (Palmgreen & Rayburn, 1979), and "social interaction" (A. M. Rubin, 1981).

Suffice it to say that it all has to do with talk. Palmgreen et al. (1980) defined interpersonal utility as "getting information which is perceived as useful in discussions with others" (p. 170). They found that one of the top two gratifications obtained from television news information is its social value. They conceived of this in terms of people watching TV news to support their viewpoints to other people, to pass on information to other people, and to furnish themselves with interesting things to talk about. In fact, these three statements all had some of the strongest positive correlations with gratifications obtained from television news viewing ($r = .68$, $r = .64$, $r = .69$, respectively; $p < .001$) among all of the dimensions investigated. In other words, people like to watch TV news because it facilitates their social interactions.

A. M. Rubin (1981) believed that one of the motivations to watch television is that it gives people something to do together. It is seen as a mechanism that clusters people in the same place and gives them something to talk about. Even if people view programs in different places it still fosters subsequent communication. Although social interaction was conceived as being a primary motivating factor for watching TV, Rubin's (1981) study resulted in ranking this dimension at 8 out of 9. Social utility may have ranked toward the bottom in this study because celebrity news was not investigated. Recall, in our society celebrity gossip shows and magazines are chart toppers. This is largely because of the topics it gives people in conversations with others.

In a later study on television gratifications and uses, A. M. Rubin (1983) achieved slightly different results. Here he reported that social interaction (i.e., hanging with friends and family, and having conversations with them) was firmly in the middle of the motivating factors to watch TV. He found that people like to utilize television as a means for social contact and communication. Again, this study did not focus on celebrity news which may have increased the overall mean score and ranking in regard to interpersonal utility and motivation to watch. The specific television content was not addressed and thus leaves a question as to how these various motivational factors would play out in a study focused on celebrity-centered news programming.

Viewer needs and motives have been widely studied in terms of social gratifications. Compesi (1980) found that one of the main reasons viewers watch soap operas was because it gives them something to talk about with other people. They talk about the plot, the action, the characters motives and behaviors, and even speculate on what is going to happen next. Greenberg, Neuendorf, Buerkel-Rothfuss, and Henderson (1982) reported that regular soap viewers watch because it helps them deal with problems with friends and family. In discussing viewer's motives, A. M. Rubin (1985) says that people watch soaps largely because of its interactive function. He says that in regard to soaps and social utility people are "seeking to meet or spend time with other persons and to acquire topics for subsequent conversation" (p. 254). Stated succinctly, A. M Rubin (1985) concluded that one of the primary motives for watching soap operas has to do with social interaction reasons.

In studying the gratifications obtained from viewing soaps, Woods (as cited in Greenberg & Woods, 1999) predicated that one reason high school girls watch is because it gives them something to talk about with friends, but not something many want to talk about with family. Perse and A. M. Rubin (1988) and Babrow (1987) also have professed that one of the top reasons people like to watch soaps is because of the social interactive gratifications they receive from it. Greenberg and Woods (1999) asserted that social interaction and social utility is not only a sought gratification of adolescent viewers, but is also a primary motive for adults as well. They argued that adults of all ages utilize soaps as a way to share time with others and to have something to talk about.

Although no research to date has been conducted in terms of the social uses of following celebrity court cases it makes sense that these utilities would be very similar to soap opera viewing. Both of them provide topics for conversation, involve interpersonal communication, and revolve around famous, or at least well-known, persons. Soap actors are celebrities. You could be sure if a leading player from *General Hospital* or from *The Young and the Restless* was arrested and subsequently faced a criminal charge it would be headline news and millions of Americans (and other nationalities) would follow it. Interpersonal communication, or talk, is a fundamental motivating factor with respect to why people are interested in celebrity court cases. Being hip and up-to-date means knowing about and being able to talk about the lives of celebrities. In a postmodern society that is fixated on pop culture and famous people this is *the* best way to demonstrate one's social fitness.

Daniel, a 21 year old aspiring journalist:

The time is 2 AM, on an average night, and the caffeine from my diet coke is still pulsing throughout my body. I turn off all the lights in my room, get under the covers, put my head to my pillow and wait. I wait for that moment when all my thoughts will stop whizzing in and out of my conscious and I will fall asleep. But that moment doesn't come soon enough. I ponder, "Do I lay awake in bed and wait for that moment of slumber to come, or do I succumb to the power that is the television?" Ultimately the television wins me over; flipping back and forth, passing through channels of infomercials until I find something of substance to watch. What will it be tonight, the History Channel, or E!, where I can catch-up on the latest celebrity gossip. This is an ordinary evening.

Lewis, a 29 year old self-proclaimed bum:

I love to know the facts about these cases [celebrity], because they are great conversation starters. I know I'm not the only one, but I love to gossip and talk about pop stars. These pop stars seem to be on top of the world, yet still continue to do dumb things ordinary people should be doing. Many people including myself will gather at the water dispenser at work, and talk about Brittney [Britney] Spears, Robert Black etc. mess up their lives [sic]. Gossip keeps this world we live in [sic], the entertainment is not scripted like a television show. Its total reality.

Tammy, a 63 year old housewife:

When walking anywhere or even standing in line at the grocery store I see adds of celebrities, the latest style file guides [sic], new weight loss programs, and the gossip columns about what the latest celebrity had done or has not done. Media is every where [everywhere] and we all can not help but be engulfed into the flame and smoke of all the gossip.

Chapter 11
Celebrities, Rodeo Drive,
and
Just Deserts
(at Spagos of course)

Justice

Of all the factors to consider when attempting to "cast a net" around the psychology behind why people watch, or read about, high-profile celebrity court cases, *justice* is probably the most unique to the current study. The other factors discussed earlier have been proposed, in varying forms and clusters, in previous studies on programs and content dealing with violent media, television news, soap operas, etc., but none has included justice as a primary motivating factor. What makes justice a central ingredient in the current study is the fact that this project is focusing on issues that fundamentally deal with the legal system and court cases. These are not fictional cases, but are very real and involve real defendants (if criminal), real lawyers, real judges, and real witnesses. To top it off, the consequences and outcomes of these cases are also real, and have real social effects (think Rodney King).

It will be argued here that one of the primary reasons that audiences follow celebrity court cases is to see that justice is served. Whether a particular celebrity defendant (if criminal) is exonerated of a charge, or charges, or is convicted is not of importance. What matters is the particular disposition that an audience member takes and the attributions that he or she assigns to the particular celebrity in each particular case. In other words, "justice" is in the eye of the beholder. Some audience members thought justice was served when O. J. Simpson was found not guilty of double homicide, while others were outraged at the verdict. Either way, people are largely motivated to pay attention to these high-profile cases because people have a need to know that they live in a just society (or at least want to believe that they live in a just society) that has a just legal system.

Justice may be thought of as what is fair and appropriate (Raney & Bryant, 2002). Zillman (1998) explicated the meaning of justice as a cognitive activity where people ponder deservedness and reflect on ethical principles. He also asserted that although there is a general sense of what constitutes justice, judgments concerning any particular situation vary greatly and that people differ with regard to basal morality (Zillman, 2000c). Justice has also been explained as "knowledge of principles of fairness," which "enables people to predict and control the consequences of their own behavior and the behavior of others" (Schmitt & Maes, 2006). These authors believed that an understanding of what is considered just allows people to avoid punishment, receive rewards, minimize negative outcomes, and maximize positive outcomes by simply obeying the rules of any given society.

An injustice is stripping one of his or her legal rights (Mill, 1957). This stands in direct contrast with justice, which is assuring one's rights are protected. Justice is activated by righting an injustice (Raney & Bryant, 2002). Evans (1981) said that in media an injustice is usually criminal and the punishment for the crime is the way of righting the wrong. He said that when a criminal gets what he or she deserves then justice has prevailed. With this in mind, justice may be thought of as both the rights of the individual and the means and methods of assuring justice. Darley and Pittman (2003) conceive of justice as falling into two general classes, one concerns the individual who was wronged, the other concerns the perpetrator. They said:

> The first class of justice-providing transactions is focused on compensation for the victim. Here the desire is to come as close as is possible to restoring victims to the state in which they were before the harm was inflicted. The second class of justice-providing transactions is more concerned with punishment, with inflicting the appropriate punishment on the perpetrators for the wrongness of their actions in inflicting the original harm. (p. 325)

What can be ascertained from this is that audiences are most likely watching these cases to see that justice is served on all fronts. Raney and Bryant (2002) supported this assertion when they claimed that people desire to see the "good guy/gal" prevail (victim compensation) and the "bad guy/gal" suffer (perpetrator punishment). Zillman (1991) referred to this moral judgment as "justice restoration."

If "justice" is in the eye of the viewer then this concept must be broken down into its specific elements. Different viewers may be looking for different forms of justice and have differing ideas about where, when, and if justice was served at all. Part of this process involves the *framing* of the court case by the media. Framing in this sense refers to the process by which the media construct news stories. These stories are strategically presented by the journalists, who choose from multiple vantage points and voices (Shah, Watts, Domke, & Fan, 2002), and the media organizations themselves, by selecting which stories to cover out of many to choose from (McQuail, 1994). Gitlin (1980) referred to media framing as the packaging and efficient relaying of information to audiences. Entman (1993) elaborates on framing by saying that daily news frames organize everyday reality and serves the intent of the sender. In this sense, media has a strong impact on constructing social reality. McQuail (1994) summed up by stating that the media frames images of reality in predictive and patterned ways. These "frames" will shape and influence how the audiences see and feel about any given high-profile court cases. Justice may be in the eye of the beholder, but that "eye" has a media-tainted contact lens on it. Everything seen on television or read in newspapers has been filtered through the framing process. Justice, it seems, is another part of our mass-mediated world.

James, a 59 year old electrician:

What attracts me to these celebrity court cases is to see that justice is being served properly to these celebrities, and that their [they are] not getting treated anymore [sic] differently then [than] any other person who is not of celebrity status. If justice is being served properly it helps me feel secure with the world around me, and that there is some good still left in this world.

Nicolette, a 32 year old mother:

I like to watch court cases partly because I have a sincere appreciation for the justice system.

Rigo, a 38 year old factory worker:

By watching [celebrity cases] it fulfills the understanding of how our justice system works. Justice is not based on the popularity of an individual but rather a rule of law that is applicable to all individuals. It seems as if these court case celebrities are undermining the justice system. Ordinary criminals are prosecuted under the law, however, a celebrity, due to its resources can basically, "pay off the law," or have the best representation. I'm not saying that no celebrity has ever served time but rather the time that a celebrity serves is inadequate to what the law is and how a normal person is convicted. If everyone had "Celebrity" representation, then less [more] people in society would most likely not be convicted [there would be fewer convictions].

Enrique, a 23 year old college student:

I find myself accepting that celebrities will always beat the justice system, and the result will always be the same.

Dick, an 83 year old World War II vet:

I am most interested in the results or final decisions in these [celebrity] cases to determine (in my mind) if the truth has been disclosed or if the punishment or non-punishment was warranted. In other words to see if justice is carried out.

Eric, a 39 year old human factors researcher:

I am more interested in the process than the people participating.

Saul, a 39 year old graduate student:

My interest in celebrity court cases is because I like to see if the justice system is as severe with famous people as with regular people. Since I was a child, I have learned that money and a known last name could get you almost anywhere you want it [sic]. I as a [an] adult can assure that this affirmation is completely true. Our justice system absolutely breaks apart under the media pressure, and that is I think [sic], one of the reasons famous people, they sometimes love to bring their personal lives into the public eye.

Just World and the Justice Motive

One of the reasons people may follow a celebrity court case is to see what kind of a world they live in: Is it safe, predictable, fair? Lerner (1977) developed his theory on a *just world* by demonstrating that people want to live in a world where people get what they deserve, and deserve what they get. A just world deems that good things should happen to good people and bad things should happen to bad people. Lerner (1977) believed that the belief in a just world is derived from two basic generalizations; first, that people generalize from concrete to abstract principles, and, second, that people generalize from their own reasoning and behavior to the reasoning and behavior of other people.

This sets up what Lerner (1977) called the *personal contract* and the *social contract*. The personal contract involves the individual understanding how he or she is supposed to behave and in return will benefit with things such as academic success, friendship, and social approval. Here, it is argued, that when a person does not live up to the personal contract he or she will pay the cost both personally and socially. The understanding of the personal contract comes from social learning, or socialization. He said that:

People learn to care about justice in familiar ways. They internalize the rules of behavior, develop a set of beliefs about themselves and society through their association with various outcomes – success-failure, positive-negative reinforcement. The consistent pattern of outcomes reinforces ways of reacting. These habits are then imbued with the value of the associated outcomes. Whether we consider them cognitions, beliefs, attitudes, sentiments, values, self-concept, what we learn and believe is essentially the reflection of the goals and the organization of our experiences provided for us by our social environment. (p. 2)

With this socialization in mind, the individual, when confronted with an injustice, will acknowledge the injustice and want to see justice restored (Maes, 1994). This may account for one of the motivations behind why people get so involved in media-covered court cases; that is, to see a violation of the personal contract righted. Lerner (2003) stipulated that the individual's justice motive stems from explicit reasoning where justice must be restored, and implicit processing where the individual may act impulsively, aggress against the transgressor, or act defensively (e.g., blaming the victim).

   If groups and society are to function successfully then the belief in justice, and
operation of justice, is a fundamental precondition (Schmitt & Maes, 2006). People must
adhere to the personal contract and have faith in the social contract. The social contract
basically stipulates that the controlling social institutions will ensure that people get what
they deserve. Lerner (1977) used legal justice as an example of the social contract. He
said that the justice of laws and the courts, which are based on equity, parity, and need,
are established and employed to determine what the deservedness is of any person in any
given encounter. People may watch unfolding court cases to ensure that the social
contract is being upheld. Even though the viewer is not an influential agent in the court
proceedings he or she is still driven by the justice motive. This is in sync with Lerner's
(2003) assertion that: "The observers cared so much about believing that people get what
they deserve and deserve what they get, that if they cannot restore justice by their actions,
they will try to do so by other means" (p. 390).

   The justice motive carries over into media news and entertainment. Justice is a core
human need, and "the arousal and subsequent satisfaction of the justice need is a
powerful entertainment tool that will be employed regularly by a large variety of media"
(Schmitt & Maes, 2006, p. 275). Mikula, Scherer, and Athenstaedt (1998) argued that
few themes may have the ability to generate such emotional arousal and suspense as does
that of justice. Z. Rubin and Peplau (1973) studied justice in fairy tales where the theme
was always about goodness winning and badness losing. They proposed that these stories
contribute to the development of children's understanding of, desire for, and belief in, a
just world.

   Raney (2002, 2003) detailed the themes of justice which can be found in all genres
of motion pictures (e.g., Westerns, action, criminal trial dramas). W. I. Miller (1998)
identified revenge and equity as common themes in narratives concerning justice. He
wrote: "The modern revenge film is about justice, doing justice" (p. 170). The belief in a
just world carries over into all media content including sports and news. Zillman et al.
(1998) posited that the justice motive is a fundamental reason why people take an interest

Tom, a 36 year old postal worker:

   *I like to watch celebrity trials to see if they get busted or not. Usually they don't.
   They have lots of money. This usually gets you out of trouble as opposed to poorer
   people. They can afford expensive lawyers, and they can get them off or get them
   a light sentence. Like O. J. and Michel Jackson. Anyone else would have went to
   prison for doing that.*

Figure 8. Illustration of justice and how audience members employ the media to ensure that their beliefs in fairness and the law are carried out in society. The media in this sense serves a surveillance function for the viewing public.

in current events and news stories. They believe that the need for justice is what motivates people to tune in, and stay tuned in to stories about injustice. This makes sense when you think about the content in most newspapers and news programs (e.g., murder, arson, wars, violence, drugs…).

Raney and Bryant (2002) believed that people follow media drama to reinforce their beliefs in a just world. They penned that "the macrostory of all drama seems to be that all injustice necessarily results in some restoration of justice" (p. 404). This restoration of justice is going to be mediated by how the narrative is framed and the audience member will not be satisfied until the wrong has been righted (Brewer, 1996b; Raney, 2002). Raney and Bryant (2002) proposed a model of crime drama that addresses framing and mediated justice, which relies heavily on empathy with the victim, viewer's punitiveness, and viewer's vigilantism. This mediated justice and sense of deservedness (Schmitt & Maes, 2006) depends upon the "degree of correspondence between the viewer's sense of justice and the statement about justice made in the drama" (Raney & Bryant, 2002, p. 407). The justice motive relates to mediated communication of justice narratives. These "justice episodes" contribute to solidifying, shaping, and validating the personal contracts of the audience and their beliefs in a just world (Lerner, 2003; Schmitt & Maes, 2006). Celebrity court cases are news-mediated events. There is good reason to suspect that the belief in a just world and the justice motive is at the core of *why people watch*.

Jose, a 37 year old government worker:

Knowing that justice was served will help me sleep better at night. In Michael Vick's example, why would I care if he was to be thrown in jail or set free? It is quite simple really. First of all, he tortured animals for his simple enjoyment.... His two year sentence gave me great joy and satisfaction even though he deserved much more. Watching these cases fulfills many needs.

Jessica, a 35 year old public health worker:

We are all knowledgeable of the crimes they [celebrities] are able to get away with (i.e. O. J. Simpson, Michael Jackson, Robert Blake, and Lane Garrison) as opposed to Lionel Tate, who at the age of twelve beat and stomped to death a playmate half his age in Florida and was charged with a life sentence. Once in a while, I feel a celebrity is made an example of and given a harsher punishment than deserved.

Allison, a 61 year old educator:

You see all these wonderful people getting severely punished for something small then you see celebrities making huge mistakes and getting nothing. It makes me sick. I want to see them get what they deserve and be treated like all other "normal" people in the world. You always hear "celebrities are just like you and me." However, this never seems true in the courtroom.

Moe, a 23 year old college student and activist:

One reason [I like to watch celebrity trials] is because I like to see how celebrities and the rich, is [are] treated differently from the poor and the middle class. My belief is that in America you can almost get away with anything if you have money. From what I have seen so far is that if a celebrity is charged with a crime, and the average person is charged with that same crime the court system would be more sympathetic to the celebrity. An example of this would be the Paris Hilton case. Never in my life have I seen someone have a jail sentence, and the court system allow that person to get out of jail early.

Rick, a 24 year old law student:

I think you want to see justice carried out and I tune in to see if celebrities get "special treatment."

Just Deserts and Retributive Justice

When a celebrity is caught up in a legal case they have often been accused of a wrongful act (e.g., Paris Hilton, driving under the influence; Phil Spector, murder). In our society when an individual deviates from socially acceptable (or legally acceptable) behaviors they have violated the social contract, and sanctions are expected to be imposed upon them. Even in a postmodern society where the media dominates mental life and celebrities are worshipped like gods, nobody, in theory, is above the law. When a famous person breaks the law people want to see justice served, and this means that the guilty party must pay for his or her wrongdoings.

There are two broad classifications of punishment. The first is utilitarian (or consequentialist) and the second is deservedness (or retributivist). The utilitarian perspective is a deterrent approach that argues that punishment for a past offence will hinder any future offenses by demonstration of commitment to laws. Jeremy Bentham (as cited in Darley, Carlsmith, & P. H. Robinson, 2000) developed the contemporary deterrence rationale which stipulates that punishment for an offense should be as, and only as, sufficient enough to deter future instances of the offense. Although deterrence is an honorable plan its effects have been minimal (Carlsmith, Darley, & P. H. Robinson, 2002). P. H. Robinson and Darley (1997) cited some statistics on why the deterrence approach is weak:

> Of the offences reported, clearance rates (the rate at which police identify and arrest a suspect for reported offences) have been steadily dropping for decades. The homicide clearance rate nationwide, which was 93% in 1955, has steadily declined to a current 67%. Rape has declined from 79% to 52%. Burglary went from a not very high 32% to a sad 13%. And, of course, getting arrested is a far cry from punishment. The overall conviction rate of those arrested for the most serious offences—homicide, rape, robbery, burglary, aggravated assault—is 30%. Further, less than half of those convicted of a felony are sentenced to prison. The cumulative effect of the many escape hatches leaves a deterrent threat that looks like this: Homicide offers a 44.7% chance of being caught, convicted, and imprisoned for that offence. A person contemplating a rape faces a 12% chance of going to prison for that offence. Robbery presents a 3.8% chance. Assault, burglary, larceny, and motor vehicle are each a 100-to-1 shot. To put it mildly, our potential offender may not be entirely cowed by the threats. (p. 4)

These authors are making the basic point that deterrence is not a very effective approach. Nagin (1998) disagreed by decrying that deterrence theory assumes that the potential criminal is a rational actor that will conduct a cost-benefit analysis prior to committing the offense and this will ultimately make the offense an unattractive option.

Deterrence, as one of the two broad categories of justifying punishment, is not believed to be a significant factor that contributes to audience motivation to follow celebrity court cases. In other words, people do not watch a media covered case on CNN in hopes that this case will deter future crime. In fact, in a study with 117 Princeton University students, the researchers Carlsmith et al. (2002) found that only 16% looked to deterrence as an answer; the rest looked to the second punishment justification known as *just deserts*.

Just deserts, or retribution, comprise the principles that determine when, how, and for what moral rationales an offender is punished (Miller, 2001; Vidmar, 2001). Sanctions for the perpetrator include retaliation and vengeance by the target or his or her kin, formal sentencing according to law by a moral authority, and/or punishment by the group to which the offender belongs (Schmitt & Maes, 2006). The motive for punishment here is to hold people accountable for their wrongdoings and make them pay for their past behavior (Vidmar, 2002). This retributionist stance is often thought of as social revenge and "as a vindictive and retrograde motive for punishment, stemming from the old and barbaric *lex talionus* rule of 'an eye for an eye'" (Darley & Pittman, 2003).

The contemporary just deserts rationale is rooted in the writings of Immanuel Kant, which was based off of the Aristotelian views that offenders should not be rehabilitated, but punished and penalized (Darley et al. 2000; Kant, 1952). Kant (1952), in his belief that people should get what they deserve wrote that "punishment can never be administered merely as a means for promoting another good" and is best to be "pronounced over all criminals proportionate to their internal wickedness" (p. 397). This punitive stance is what serves to protect the members of society against antisocial transgressions (Vermunt & Steensma, 1991). Schmitt (1996) said that members of a society share a common interest in preserving order and social norms, and this can only be accomplished by raising the costs and lessening the benefits of moral deviations by members of the group. He waxed: "Retaliation and retributive actions to unjust treatment are an effective and typical way to raise the cost to the victimizer" (p. 5).

Criminal law is at the core of establishing and maintaining social consensus on what is moral and normative. If millions of people are watching criminal trials on television then this is most likely creating some consensus on right and wrong behavior and the expectations associated with these beliefs. P. H. Robinson and Darley (1997) argued that the criminal law's most influential social effects lies in its ability to build, shape, and maintain societal norms and moral principles. This "deontological moral mandate" is rooted in our desert-based liability system where we assign blame, liability, and punishment according to the principles of justice and moral outrage (Darley et al. 2000; Elster, 1990).

In discussing retribution toward the perpetrator of the harm and society's need to punish, LaFave (2000) scripted that:

> it has been argued with some force that the only real basis for distinction between crimes and civil wrongs lies in the moral condemnation which the community visits upon the criminal but not (at least not so powerfully) upon his civil wrongdoer counterpart. (p. 12)

The argument is that compensation to the victim, or to society, is not enough. Darley and Pittman (2003) noted that "people feel that suitable punishment must be inflicted on the perpetrator by the judicial system, a punishment in proportion to the moral gravity of the offense committed" (p. 326). Think of the O. J. Simpson murder trial. The Goldmans won the civil case against Simpson (compensation) but this did not satisfy the Goldmans or many members of society. What the Goldmans, and millions of viewing Americans, really wanted was punishment (retribution) for his alleged wrongful acts.

It appears that what most Americans want in terms of punishment is just-deserts, or righting a wrong (P. H. Robinson & Darley, 1995, 1997). The goal is to assess the magnitude of harm and subsequently conceive a punishment that is proportionate in severity, "if not in kind" (Kahneman, Schkade, & Sunstein, 1998; Rossi, Berk, & Campbell, 1997). Carlsmith et al. (2002) reported in a study on motivation to punish that just deserts accounted for 76% of the philosophical justification to bring an offender to justice. They concluded that unless a punishment is imposed upon the offender that there is a sense that justice has not been done. This need for justice is generally served by a just deserts perspective where "a just society is one that assigns just deserts punishments proportionate to the moral blameworthiness of the offense, and it must not fail to punish wrongdoing in these ways" (Carlsmith et al., 2002, p. 297). To rephrase, it has generally been found that when people are making sentencing decisions, that is, when they are considering the punishment that should be given to the transgressor, the just deserts perspective is the one almost exclusively employed (Carlsmith et al. 2002; Oswald, Hupfeld, Klug, & Gabrial, 2002).

The assumption in the current study is that audience members do not follow celebrity court cases with deterrence in mind. They become engaged because they want to see an offender, if believed to be guilty, punished for his or her transgressions. Audience members wish to see justice handed down, even to those that are famous, from a retributivist standpoint. A recent poll on Tru TV resulted in over 85% of the voting audience saying that they would like to see Phil Spector found guilty and sent to prison for the murder of Lana Clarkson. It is a safe bet to say that these audience members were coming from the just deserts perspective and wanted to see Spector punished for his crime in proportion to the severity of his offense. Compensation would not be enough. According to the literature, (e.g., Carlsmith et al. 2002; French, 2001; Tyler & Weber, 1983) people by and large want law-breakers to pay for their crimes. Through these just desert punishments, or retributions, a sense of normalcy is restored, and members of society take solace in the belief that justice was served.

Danny, a 44 year old media programmer:

I am a firm believer that people should be held responsible for their actions. It is nice to see when celebrities are punished just like everyone else.

Shih, a 22 year old foreign exchange student:

I want to discover how they will be treated in the courts... I am wondering if there will be any exception for famous people to escape from the reality's judge [a real judge and not a fake one seen in TV dramas]. To me, this is an unfair world and an unfair society, so I really seek I can see the fair judge from these famous cases [a fair ruling] and those cases will lead people a right view to judge this world through justice [fair trial] ....justice becomes the goal I seek for.

Distributive Justice

Audience members may also be likely to be motivated to follow a celebrity court case to see if celebrities are getting a "fair shake" in the fines, sentences, probation terms, etc. that are handed down to them from the courts. For example, in a high-profile celebrity breakup (e.g., Alec Baldwin and Kim Bassinger; Denise Richards and Charlie Sheen) are the terms of the divorce fair for both sides? Are the courts basing decisions on need and equity? In criminal trials are celebrities receiving special treatment? Are they getting what may be referred to here as *celebrity court justice*, where they are handed unusually light sentences, or given third or fourth chances to correct bad behavior (think Britney Spears)? It seems reasonable to infer that a motivating factor involved in this phenomenon revolves around people's need to see if others are getting fair allocation; and this includes celebrities.

Distributive justice has to do with the fairness of outcome (Schmitt, 1996; Schmitt & Sabbagh, 2004). This "fairness" is based on judgments on whether the courts have acted in a satisfactory manner in deciding on things such as fines, sentencing, terms, etc. (D. T. Miller, 2001; Elster, 1992). Determining whether a case outcome is just or unjust is influenced by various sources. These sources would include: comparison with earlier court cases, outcomes received by others, defendant evaluations of their own sentences compared to others convicted of the same crime, and evaluation based on principled criterion (Casper, Tyler, & Fisher, 1988).

In a court case, perceived fairness will have a great deal to do with final distribution, which is based heavily on long-standing social norms and institutions (Lind, Kurtz, Musante, Walker, & Thibaut, 1980). If the average person goes to jail for one month for a driving under the influence conviction, the question generated becomes: Is a famous person convicted of the same offense going to get the same outcome? Or is that famous person going to receive celebrity court justice? Thibaut and Walker (1975) proposed that sentiments about case outcomes would be seen as most fair when the decision is made by an impartial third party. In celebrity court cases this would usually involve an unbiased judge, not one that is starstruck, or one that is hell-bent on showing that he or she is not swayed by fame and goes on the warpath (e.g., the judge that overruled the Los Angeles County Sheriff and threw Paris Hilton back in jail with an even harsher sentence).

Tyler (1984) argued that feelings about distributive justice involve attitudes toward the judges involved in cases. He said that people are primarily concerned with whether or not a particular judge is handing down comparable outcomes to different defendants. If not, then people become "angry" with the system and feel as though the system is unjust. Sarat (as cited in Tyler, 1984) concluded that it is "the perception of unequal treatment [which] is the single most important source of popular dissatisfaction with the American legal system" (p. 55). D. T. Miller (2001) concurred with this statement by mentioning that one of the most common means of assessing distributive justice is by examining the rules and reactions of others, allocation, and equality. If allocation is not fair and if people are not treated equally then there will be an overall sense of injustice. This feeling of injustice is an attitudinal response. Lind et. al. (1990) supported this by pointing out, "Perceived justice and outcome satisfaction appear to be determined largely by subjective expectations and impressions rather than by objective features of litigation" (p. 986). Audience members at home are clearly going to be affected by their subjective feelings toward the particular celebrity (i.e., their dispositions and attributions). These attitudes are going to weigh in heavily concerning their feelings about any particular case outcome.

Judgments of distributive fairness and case disposition has a good deal to do with equity. *Equity theory* assumes that outcomes across recipients are universal, and any deviation from this principle causes distress, anger, and indignation (Schmitt & Maes, 2006; Schmitt & Sabbagh, 2004). Personality factors will also influence attitudes toward outcome (Major & Deaux, 1982). Huseman, Hatfield, and Miles (1985) proposed that people are often *equity sensitive* and want to ensure that people get what they are entitled to, or deserve (if being punished). This personality may also account for why some people follow celebrity court cases; they want to see that the principle of equity is being upheld in our legal system.

Equity theory would be concerned with the act committed, the punishment given, and outcome expectancy relative to others and the past (Deutsch, 1985; Törmblom, 1992). Schmitt (1996) conjectured that the most fundamental justice criterion that individuals apply to any given social context is proportionality of input and outcome across individuals. In other words, people should get what they need (e.g., welfare), what they deserve (e.g., punishment), or receive equitable returns based on what they have put in (e.g., divorce). Equity basically revolves around feelings of fair rewards, or fair outcomes. That is, are people being treated the same in regard to what they are getting?

People are watching high-profile cases partly because they want to see that justice is served in terms of distributive outcomes. People want to know that their liked celebrities are being treated fairly during the duration of a legal case. They will make sentimental judgments and make comparisons to other celebrity cases to check on equality (e.g., the endless comparisons made between the driving under the influence cases of Lindsay Lohan, Paris Hilton, and Nicole Richie). Schmitt and Maes (2006) expressed that the principle of equality, in terms of distributive justice, is one of the most basic things that people consider when evaluating the fairness of outcomes. The basic question becomes: Are celebrities being treated the same as everyone else in the legal system, or is there such a thing as celebrity court justice? People want to know, and this is a contributing factor in regard to why people watch.

Janice, a 49 year old rock climber:

> *Justice is very important to me. I watch [celebrity cases] for justice because I like to look at the progress that is being made when we look at things like fair trials. I want to see if someone would get off easy because they are rich. Or [if] someone would have a hard time because of their race.*

Procedural Justice

> *All I know is just what I read in newspapers.*
> American humorist Will Rogers

If audience members were only concerned with case outcomes then one might guess that they would only tune in to see the verdict by a jury or ruling of a judge. But this is not the case. People get involved in celebrity trials right from the beginning and stay involved all the way to the end; and then some. People are clearly interested in the entire workings of the legal system, and also how the celebrity is dealing with his or her legal troubles. One might venture to say that people are concerned with *how* a case unfolds, and *how* a judgment is rendered. This, in part, will contribute to the perceptions of fairness in any given case.

Procedural justice is the concern with the decision-making process, not the outcome (Schmitt & Maes, 2006). Lind and Tyler (1988) described procedural justice as the fairness of mechanisms, processes, and methods used to determine outcomes, rather than the fairness of outcomes themselves. Leventhal (1976) believed that people are fundamentally concerned with fair procedures. He said that these procedures are instrumental in nature because the pursuit of principles of procedural justice is believed to maximize the party's outcomes which are rooted in certain criteria. This, Leventhal (1976) argued, is what determines whether or not a person feels a procedure and outcome is just.

The earliest scholars to study the concept of procedural justice in a legal context were Thibaut and Walker (1975, 1978). They contended that procedural justice consists of two broad components made up of process control and outcome control. Process control, they suggested, has to do with the fairness of the procedures by which outcomes are distributed. In other words, they believed that it is the process itself that largely determines the outcome of any given case. They further suggested that even if a case outcome is not completely favorable, citizens will support the decision so long as it was based in fair procedures. Think of the common question: "Did he get a fair trial?" This question is grounded in ideas about fair process.

Thibaut and Walker's (1975, 1978) findings have been supported in several studies linking satisfaction with outcomes to judgments about fair procedures (e.g., McFarlin & Sweeney, 1992; Schmitt & Dorfel, 1999; Tyler, Degoey, & Smith, 1996). Lind et. al. (1990) studied tort litigants' judgments of procedures and their satisfaction with the outcome of their case and found that:

> Procedural justice judgments are heavily influenced by subjective assessments of the procedures and that outcome satisfaction depends more on expected than on objective outcomes….Perceived justice and outcome satisfaction appear to be determined largely by subjective expectations and impressions rather than by objective features of litigation. (pp. 985-986)

This idea that tort litigants' perceptions of procedural fairness and their expectations of outcomes and costs as being grounded in certain criteria fits with Thibaut and Walker's (1975, 1978) conception.

In a later study on adjudication procedure and the effects of procedures on attitudes toward an adjudicated outcome, Lind et al. (1980) concluded that they found "unambiguous evidence" that the perceived fairness of an adversarial procedure is rooted in perceptions of nonbias in the judge's decision. They argued that the laws and rules concerning the procedure by which case outcomes are handed down heavily influences acceptance and perceived fairness of those outcomes. Thus, reactions to adjudicated resolutions are mediated by perceptions related to process control and fairness. Lind et al. (1980) stated that "process control refers to control over the arguments and evidence to be considered in a conflict resolution session or hearing, whereas decision control refers to the power to specify and enforce a resolution of the conflict" (pp. 643-644). Again, this is right in line with Thibaut and Walker's (1975, 1978) assertion that procedures for resolving conflicts over outcomes will be most satisfactory when the process places control in the hands of the disputants and decisional control in the hands of an impartial, unbiased third party (e.g., a judge, a litigator).

In a legal case, process control seen as the extent and nature of control an individual has over the presentation of evidence (Tyler, 1994). This has been broken down into concerns about neutrality (nonbias), equity, the respect for rights, fair treatment, dignity, and trust in the motives of the third-party authority (Tyler, 1989, 1994). Casper, Tyler, and Fisher (1988) studied procedural justice in felony and found that litigants' sense of fair treatment during the trial was grounded in process control; meaning their opportunity to express their point of view fully to an impartial and thoughtful maker. To convey differently, defendants will be more satisfied with the process and outcome of the trial if they have a fair shot at making their case and being heard by a trusted third party.

This is all and good but what about the audience's feelings about the procedures and outcomes of court cases? One can assume that the celebrity's reaction to a decision is going to affect the viewing audience: Remember Paris Hilton crying in the back of her mom's car, whimpering, "It's not fair!" This image was all over the media and millions of Americans were debating over whether the judge's sentence really was fair to Hilton or not. Was this a case of *reverse* celebrity justice? Was she being excessively punished because of her celebrity status? Either way this case caused a huge media frenzy and was one of the most covered stories of 2007.

Tyler (1988) conducted a study addressing how outside observers judge the fairness of a legal case. He found seven criteria by which people evaluate whether or not legal authorities act fairly. They are:

(1) The degree to which those authorities were motivated to be fair; (2) judgments of their honesty; (3) the degree to which the authorities followed ethical principles of conduct; (4) the extent to which opportunities for representation were provided; (5) the quality of the decisions made; (6) the opportunities for error correction; and (7) whether the authorities behaved in a biased fashion. (p. 103)

These seven criteria were found to heavily influence perception and satisfaction with the notion of procedural justice; along with the additional criterion of consistency in judgments across time and across people (Leventhal, 1980). It is believed here that viewers of legal cases, whether they are aware of it or not, use many or all of these criteria in making judgments of fairness about the procedures and outcomes of celebrity trials.

On a final note, it must be mentioned in more detail how audience judgments are filtered through a media angle. The media methodically structure and plan how these court cases are presented and this undoubtedly affects viewer reactions. All events in the media are structured by journalist's reports about these events and situation (McCombs, 2004) and larger organizational factors (Epstein, 2000). This shaping of attitudes and opinions is what McCombs (2004) referred to as "setting the agenda." This is where the media calls attention to some events (while ignoring others) and *plants* the salience of issues in the viewer's minds. This primes the viewer to think a certain way and place importance on certain issues (e.g., celebrity trials). According to Scheufele (1999), this framing of stories literally shapes the way people perceive an event. Shah, Watts, Domke, and Fan (2002) pointed out that the media literally set up and construct the viewer's orientation toward any given issue or event.

But the process is not just one way. Whether or not an audience member perceives a court case to have been just or unjust is largely based on motivation to watch and other psychological and cognitive variables. The event is being mediated by the networks and print publications but it is also being actively analyzed in the minds of the audience. The audience member is not in the courtroom so they must get their information through the framing process of agenda-setting. Taken together, the viewer-producer equation can be wrapped up by the following quote:

> Frequency of coverage in the news media is part of the explanation for agenda-setting effects, but only in tandem with the psychological relevance of items on the media agenda to members of the public. Public salience is the combined result of availability and personal relevance. (McCombs, 2004, p. 60)

In sum, viewer perception of the procedural fairness of a celebrity trial is a function of both their personal dispositions, attributions, needs, and motives, and how the media frame, plant, and present the case. It is a two-way process. To fully understand how it works one must grasp both sides of the equation.

Justice: Summarized

As can be gathered from reading this past passage, justice is a multi-faceted construct and involves more detail than one might originally think. People have what Lerner (1980) referred to as a "need for justice." They would like to believe, whether right or wrong, that we live in a world where people are treated fairly and get what they deserve. If people are not treated in a just manner this will tend to cause psychological discomfort and a feeling that the social contract is not being upheld. It is believed that if the governing authorities (e.g., judges), and the legal system in general, do not uphold the moral integrity of society then citizens will ultimately develop a disbelief in justice and consequently will lose their belief in the uprightness of the justice system (Arts, Hermkens, & van Wisck, 1995; Tyler & Smith, 1998).

Audience members will most likely follow a court case not just for one of the aspects but, on some level, all of them. People watching the Paris Hilton case were paying attention not just to what her sentence was going to be, but were also surveying how she was being treated prior to the decision. In other words, the viewing audience was monitoring both procedural and distributive justice. They were also focused on what her punishment would be, and should be, in light of the seriousness of the crimes committed: This is in line with the notions of the justice motive and the need for a just world. Audiences wanted to see if Hilton would have to pay for her transgressions (i.e., retribution/just deserts) or if she would receive Hollywood celebrity justice; thus annoying many people's sense of fair treatment under the law, and violating the notion of a just world.

Justice is believed to be a significant factor pertaining to why people follow celebrity court cases. This is one of the missing links in the previously developed models that focus on the needs and motives of individuals that watch news programs, soap operas, dramatic presentations, and other forms of programming. Justice is a core need for members of society. It is both a personal and social contract. People expect others to uphold justice in face-to-face encounters, and they most certainly expect the relied upon larger social institutions, such as the legal system, to uphold it morally and absolutely.

Although the survey instrument being utilized in this study for data collection was not intended to investigate justice in terms of viewing motivations it is believed here to be a core reason why people watch or read about court cases. The bulk of this project is contained in the literature review and thus serves both as a theoretical and empirical investigation. It may be thought of as both a theoretical narrative that spells out the eight primary psychological theories behind the audience member's needs and motivations, and also a quantitative probe that collects empirical data from a survey technique. Justice is a necessary part of this study and is believed to be a core reason why people are driven to follow celebrity court cases. The concluding section of this project addresses this viewing factor in terms of future theory building and empirical investigations.

Nikki, a 33 year old loan officer:

My favorite show is the People's Court. I like to see that there is justice, and there are consequences when people are mistreated or wronged.

Jenny, A 55 year old administrator:

Whenever I tune in to see a celebrity court cases it is primarily to keep an eye on our justice system. I hate it when famous people get off for their crimes. Everyone should be treated equally. But this is not always the case.

Sammy "The Bull," a 62 year old medical supplies distributor and social critic:

If the charges are egregious (i.e: the Phil Spector murder trial), then I will read the trial, predominantly to learn the facts as presented in court. I will periodically "check in" with the case as it progresses....My interest in the case is primarily this: Is the accused very wealthy/powerful? Are the facts in evidence overwhelming against the accused? My interest is always to learn how the "justice system" functions in the case of the walthy and powerful vs. how it operates in the cases of a common citizen who is accused of a similar offense.... If the defendant is convicted, then my interest is to discover what sentence the court gives to a wealthy and powerful criminal. vs. what sentence is given to a common citizen who is convicted of an identical crime....Justice is my top reason [for] following celebrity court cases] because the jurisprudence system does not operate in a vacuum. I am a student of history and am keenly aware of the role played by those with wealth and power. Outcomes in court cases are ALWAYS impacted heavily by the socio/economic and educational background of the defendant. The poor are always at greater risk, for the obvious reason that they do not have the resources, financial and otherwise, to marshal an effective defense in a court of law, compared with a defendant who has wealth and power.

Chapter 12
Synthesis of the Theoretical Model:
Why We Watch (or Read, or Listen, or...)

The Psychology of the Audience

The purpose of the last eight chapters was to demonstrate how complex the motives of the viewing audience really are. People are not mindless and passive. They engage the media because it helps to fulfill certain social and psychological needs, and it also rewards them with certain gratifications. But these various components are not separated from one another; in fact, they are consanguineous and interconnected. It is not the purpose here to try and show that one need or motive is isolated from other needs and motives. The purpose is to show that they can operate in the viewer's mind simultaneously and in harmony with one another.

A viewer can be watching a high-profile court case not just to escape boredom, but also to gather information for an upcoming social event. Another viewer may be watching to distract herself from unwanted responsibilities, *and* to feel connected to various media personae, *and* to simply be entertained; all at the same time. A third viewer may be watching for all of the above reasons *and* several more. The point is that people watch, listen to, or read about these celebrity cases for a reason and with a purpose.

The previously discussed media-related theories combine to make up the conceptual mapping being constructed in this work. There has been a vast amount of research done on understanding the scope of the constructs and the roles they play in regard to media use. This work will pull these theories and concepts into a coherent scheme that will, hopefully, capture the basic parameters associated with *why* people watch celebrity court cases. Parasocial interaction, loneliness, enjoyment, diversion, identification, social use, escape, and justice, all combine to make up the psychological composite that pertains to the audience members. This piece of literature was intended to illuminate these multiple components and to assist in conceptualizing the psychological portrait being developed in regard to the needs and motives of the viewing audience.

Figure 9 illustrates how all eight of the previously discussed social and psychological need and motivations work simultaneously and in harmony within the minds of the audience members. Again, it is not being proposed here that all eight are at play in every single audience member, or that any particular need or motivation is a dominant factor, or even a factor at all. What is being proposed is that there is a combination of reasons that people watch or read about celebrity court cases. These numerous combinations and dimensions are unique to each particular individual, each

92

particular court case, and each particular setting and context. For example, on one occasion an individual may follow a court case simply to see that justice is served and that the famous person gets his just deserts. On a different occasion that same individual may follow another court cases because she is bored and wants to be entertained. These combinations and dimensions are theoretically infinite (e.g., She could be a little bored, sort of bored, very bored, excruciatingly bored, etc.). Once again, everybody has their own unique social and psychological reasons for having an interest in watching these cases, and no two reasons (for any two people) are exactly the same.

Figure 9. A composite illustration demonstrating how the eight primary social and psychological needs and motivations can all operate simultaneously in the viewers mind.

Theoretical Findings

This book has utilized many quotes from many different individuals that participated in either survey research or moderated focus groups where the topic was centered on celebrity court cases and why people watch, read, or listen (on the radio) to them. The findings were both illuminating and contributory to the work and the further development of theory and practice. This particular project was what is known as theoretical and qualitative in orientation. (For a quantitative study that utilizes the same theoretical framework [introduction and literature review] but the methods and findings focuses on statistical analysis, please refer to *High-Profile Celebrity Court Cases: An Investigation Into Audience Uses, Needs, and Motivations*).

An interesting finding of this qualitative-theoretical writing was that four of the eight general theories seemed to "rise to the top" whereas the other four seem to play a more sub-primary role for most of the viewers. In other words, four of the eight theories appear to be a less dominating factor when considering why people like to watch these various court cases. Each of the eight will be briefly discussed and then a composite model will be presented.

Parasocial Interaction

Parasocial interaction refers to media interaction where there is an apparent quasi-relationship between spectator and performer. It is a relationship that develops over time where the friendship with a media personality is based on felt affective ties and familiarity with the media persona (Horton & Wohl, 1956; R. B. Rubin & A. M. Rubin, 2001). Parasocial interaction involves attitude similarity, identification, attraction, intimacy with, and reliance on the persona (Conway & A. M. Rubin, 1991; Eyal & A. M. Rubin, 2003). Parasocial interaction occurs largely because the audience member finds the lives of those in the media to be interesting, exciting, and/or important. In a sense, they feel as though they have an interest in the lives of those celebrities and often become attached to them on some level.

Parasocial interaction did not prove to be one of the dominant reasons that people watch or follow these cases. Only a small handful of individuals mentioned or wrote (in essay format) that this was a major reason they watch. In fact, most of the men and women who participated felt that parasocial interaction was not a reason they watch. I suspect (from my subsequent conversations with some of them) that some people think that admitting a parasocial interaction with a media persona means that you are sort of kooky in the head, or missing a few marbles. Remember, this is not what it means. Parasocial interaction can happen to anyone, even the most sane and well-adjusted of us all. It simply means that you have come to "know" a celebrity (e.g., habits, mannerism, dress, talk, etc.) and have come to expect certain things from them, certain behaviors, certain reactions, etc. A further study that spends a little more time with PSI (e.g., explaining the premise, using better survey questions) may culminate with different findings.

Escapism

Escapism refers to entering the dreamlike world of the media for substitute gratifications (Katz & Foulkes, 1962). To escape means to "leave" reality in both a cognitive and emotional way (Vorderer, 1996). People may want to escape in media for several reasons which may include boredom, alienation, shortcomings in one's life, or simply as a means of excitement and stimulation. Either way it is a means to dive into a fantasy world and imagine being somewhere else or somebody else.

Escapism also proved to be one of the "weaker" explanations as to why people follow these cases. Although escapism had a more positive response than parasocial interaction it was still one of the sub-primary four theories. I suspect that many individuals mixed up some the boundaries with diversion and subsequently weakened escapism. My thoughts on this stem from the analysis of the essays. An additional study could better distinguish the lines between the two different theories and how they serve different purposes (although there has been shown to be a fairly strong association between the two theories). With some of the participants I came to suspect that escapism to them meant a deficiency in their lives, which it does not. With this perception it stands to reason that some people would not want to acknowledge this as being a motivating factor.

Loneliness

Loneliness is "the unpleasant experience that occurs when a person's network of social relations is deficient in some important way" (Perlman & Peplau, 1981, p. 31). Loneliness can also grow out of a cognitive appraisal that one's social interaction is lacking in a qualitative way (Perse & A. M. Rubin, 1990). Loneliness may occur from a sense of being alone and may lead to depression and sadness and may incite an individual to turn to media for gratifications. Loneliness is a feeling state that may occur in those without close personal relationships. Loneliness may even occur in those with many close personal relationships but the individual still feels lonely, misunderstood, and/or depressed.

Loneliness also demonstrated to be one of the sub-dominant factors when considering this phenomenon. Although no factor discussed is unimportant (because every component was a dominant reason, or at least an important reason for some individuals) loneliness did not demonstrate to be a strong motivating factor for most of the people. My suspicion once again is that many people do not want to admit that they turn to media when they are feeling depressed or lonely; even though many studies have shown just the opposite across all demographic lines. In other words, people do turn to media when they are feeling lonely even if they cannot admit this to themselves.

Diversion

Diversion is utilizing the media to avoid taking care of unwanted responsibilities (e.g., chores, work, homework). Blumler (1979) conceived of diversion as using media to relieve oneself from boredom and the constraints of daily routines. Kim et al. (2003) saw diversion as a way to escape boredom and lose track of time. Media diversion could simply be a way to pass time. It could also be a psychological distraction to avoid thinking about bills, car problems, relationship problems, etc.

This particular theory did prove to be a central factor when considering why people watch celebrity court cases. The explanation of diversion seemed to resonate well with those surveyed. It did not seem to "threaten" them with admissions of psychological problems or maladjustments in their lives. To acknowledge that one watches court cases to pass time, or avoid doing chores, etc., seemed "normal" and did not self-implicate. This finding fits well with the literature that has studied media uses and gratifications. I believe that this component alone could merit studies in regard to media use.

Identification

Identification refers to connecting with a media celebrity on a psychic level where the audience member empathizes and relates to what they are dealing with in their lives. Identification occurs when a viewer shares the interests of another individual, has an emotional tie with another individual, or believes that he or she has a vested interest in the life of another (Fraser & Brown, 2002). Identification often involves similarity and is a process whereby the individual puts him- or herself in the place of another and experiences what that person is going through and feels (Basil, 1996; Jose & Brewer, 1984). The average person has problems and troubles, and so do celebrities and this may cause an individual to feel they have something in common with the famous person.

Identification was the last of the four sub-primary components in the theoretical model. This particular component did not prove to be all that important to most of the audience members in this study. A small handful did mention identification as being a major reason they have followed or would follow a celebrity case. Their motivations seem to stem from their capacity to relate to what the famous person is going through (legal troubles, emotional pain, etc.). There was also a clear gender difference with identification. Women appear to identify with media celebrities and empathize more with them than the men. This could be a real fact, or simply a socialized difference where men are taught not to be as caring as women and subsequently cannot display any compassion or concern to others (especially unknown others). A further study needs to be conducted that better probes this concept and its relation to audience members and media personae.

Enjoyment

Enjoyment, simply put, refers to the pleasure experienced when engaging media entertainment (Raney, 2003). Enjoyment means to be entertained by the happenings and drama in the media. This could encompass physiological arousal and excitement. Raney (2006) believed that media enjoyment is based largely around psychological and motive conditions (e.g., interest, mood management). Enjoyment also largely involves disposition, which refers to how you feel about a particular celebrity. Positive dispositions enjoy and favor positive outcomes, while negative dispositions enjoy and favor negative outcomes. Enjoyment may be thought of as the equivalent to having fun with media.

Enjoyment certainly proved to be one of the top four reasons that people follow celebrity court cases. Virtually every person responded that this plays at least some part in why they watch (although a few said that it played no part at all). The message was that these cases are fun and exciting to watch. People commonly responded that it is enjoyable to watch celebrities go through these tough court battles. Some even responded that they get a kick out of seeing them get into trouble and mess up their lives. Whatever the particular reasons, the underlying common denominator was that these cases are dramatic and suspenseful. This supports one of the core arguments made at the beginning of this book which was that these cases play into many things that human beings long for and assists in the fulfillment of several social and psychological needs. Audience enjoyment proved to be a central explanatory factor.

Social Use

Social use represents specific seeking of information that is useful in making decisions about personal or public issues (i.e., decisional utility) and general information seeking (Palmgreen et al. 1980). Social use also refers to talk, or socializing. This is where the individual uses the media as an interactive function to give them something to do with others, while at the same time it also provides topics for conversation (Greenberg & Woods, 1999; A. M. Rubin, 1983; Wenner & Gantz, 1989). Social use basically refers to utilizing the various media to give you something to talk about with others, something to do with others, for learning about society (e.g., laws, new things), for acquiring valuable information on how to proceed on something in your life (e.g., how to behave, or how not to behave, in certain circumstances), and for staying socially fit (e.g., being up on the latest trends, fashions, celebrity gossip, etc).

Social use was without question a major core component in this study's findings. This factor was mentioned by well over 90% of the audience members as playing some part in why they watch or read about celebrity court cases. Most of the audience members said that is accounts for 20% or more of the total reason they watch. A good portion even rated it as reaching 30, 40, and even 50% of the total reason they watch. It appears that people really like to follow these cases because it provides fun (and important) topics for conversations with others. Many stated that they would feel "out of the loop" and out of touch if they did not know what was going on in the media and in famous people's lives. Social use has demonstrated to be a very useful component in understanding this postmodern phenomenon.

Justice

Justice refers to what is right, or fair. Justice may be the concern with ensuring that we live in a just world where things are honest and people can be trusted (Lerner, 1980; Schmitt & Maes, 2006). Justice may mean the belief that people should get what they deserve and deserve what they get; meaning people should get their just deserts and retribution should be dished out appropriately (Miller, 2001; Raney & Bryant, 2002). In a court case justice also refers to having a fair trial (i.e., procedural justice) and receiving a fair outcome (i.e., distributive justice). The justice motive simply refers to the need to believe, or to see, that equity and fair treatment is carried out for members of society.

Justice certainly proved to be a central core ingredient in the psychological model being constructed in this book. Out of all of the eight theories being presented for this model this one is of my personal favorites in regard to this particular topic. Sitcoms are very popular, but not because of the justice motive. Soap operas are very popular, but not because of the justice motive. Sports programming is very popular, but not because of the justice motive. Celebrity court cases are very popular, *because* of the justice motive.

Although people watch these court cases for various other reasons (e.g., social use, enjoyment, identification) justice seems to prevail in regard to stimulating people's need to feel that they live in a fair world where people get what they deserve. The justice component appears to be the primary component that sparks the frontal lobe more than any of the others. It is the area that leads to debates about the law—procedural and distributive. It is the area that stimulates intellectual conversation and critical thinking more than any of the others. If it was not for the justice component then it would stand to reason that these court cases would be much less popular than they are.

Almost every individual mentioned justice (or some variation of it) as being a reason that they watch or follow high-profile court cases. The range for justice went from 0 to 90% in regard to the total reason that they watch. The most common percentage was somewhere in the 20s (20% - 30%). This numbers, along with their written essays leads me to conclude that this factor is certainly a major reason why viewers watch these cases. Additional studies focusing on this theoretical factor and this topic would certainly be useful and would shed needed light on its role pertaining to this cultural pastime. With that said, justice has cemented itself at the core of audience needs and motivations.

Criticisms of Celebrity Court Cases

Not all of the individuals expressed positive feelings about these ongoing cases. In fact, some had some very strong negative feelings about them:

Jackie, a 31 year old sociologist:

I think our culture is obsessed with the lives of celebrities for several reasons. I believe that people have become incredibly lazy and slothful in heir pursuit of knowledge and information. They lack the necessary motivation to stay current on news and world events and substitute celebrity gossip for otherwise crucial information. It seems much easier for people to stomach a dose of celebrity smut news rather than deal with a head full of Darfur genocide talk....I think the media has done a fine job of erasing our culture's ability to think for itself. We've become specialists in the art of passive consumption. Whatever the media wants to hand out is what we take; it seems that we consume it entirely without question. We are like starving feral children being thrown scraps of the most putrid paltry meat, only too crazed and stupid to know the cornucopia of food we'd be allowed of [if] we would only ask for it.

Cynthia, a 23 year old college student:

I rarely watch celebrity court cases I find them irrelevant to my life, however, sometimes when I'm channel surfing I make a quick stop to stay updated.

Jill, a 33 year old dental assistant:

I am not the type to sit down and watch celebrity court cases. They do not interest me at all. I think it might have to do with the fact that I grew up in a very poor and dangerous neighborhood where many of my childhood friends are now either incarcerated or dead. So I am too familiar with court cases and the real impact they can have in one's life.

Miles, a 70 year old retired electric worker:

I can't say that I find celebrity cases to be all that interesting. For I feel that there isn't anything more interesting then [than] my own life. It isn't to say that a news story regarding Brittney Spears were to happen to appear on my TV set, that I'd immediately rush to change the channel. News stories regarding celebrities aren't stories that I deliberately seek out. If anything, those sorts of stories seem to seek out the public in general. It is like a tidal wave that you can't avoid. No matter where you hide, the celebrity drama of the day, will find a way to find you.

Comment:

One of the interesting things that I noticed with every single criticism about the media, our culture, and these court cases was that every person ultimately wound up stating that they have watched at least some part of a high-profile court case. It appears that even when you do not want to have an interest in them you still, on some level, succumb to them through one or more of the following— social pressure, media bombardment, passing interest, boredom, etc.

Conclusion

The primary objective of this book was to illuminate the various reasons why people pay attention to these unbelievably popular celebrity court cases. At times they are more covered in the media than anything other story of the day. Why are they so popular? Why do so many people spend their time and lives watching them? What do they do for us socially? What do they do for us psychologically? What do they do for us emotionally? What needs do they serve? The intention of this book was to help to answer these questions and many more. Hopefully, on some level, it did.

The following model is gives a visual display of the working of the eight theories. They all play some part, but the top four seem to be the most dominant in this study. It was conceived to encompass the totality of why we watch. It is believed to cover the range of the social and psychological needs and motivations behind the audience's involvement in the high-profile court cases. The eight theories sort of "surround" the viewer's mind and capture what uses and gratifications are being sought and/or met by these famous trials. It does not take into considerations any deviant or aberrant motivations that some individuals may have (e.g., fetishes, delusions). It is intended to cover the psychological range that explains the general reasons why people watch these court cases. My desire is that it does just that.

The Celebrity Court Case
Psychological Model

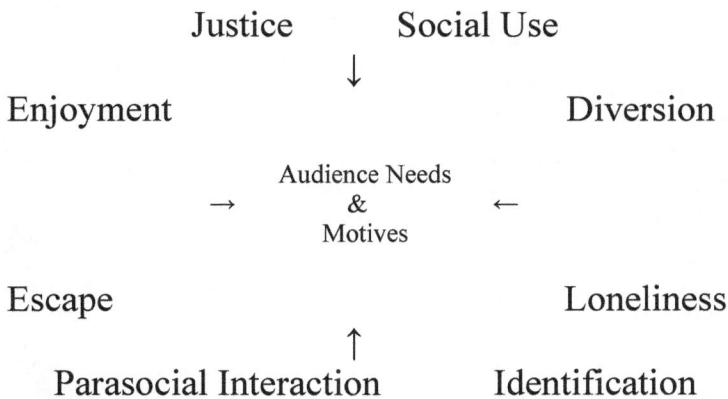

Justice   Social Use

↓

Enjoyment   Diversion

Audience Needs
→   &   ←
Motives

Escape   Loneliness

↑

Parasocial Interaction   Identification

Figure 10. The composite mapping of the eight primary psychological theories that helps to explain the range of reasons pertaining to why people pay attention to the various and ongoing media covered celebrity court cases.

References

Alexander, A. (1985). Adolescents' soap opera viewing and relational perceptions. *Journal of Broadcasting and Electronic Media, 29,* 295-308.

Alperstein, N. M. (1991). Imaginary social relationships with celebrities appearing in television commercials. *Journal of Broadcasting and Electronic Media, 35*(1), 43-58.

Altheide, D. L., & Snow, R. P. (1979). *Media logic.* Beverly Hills, CA: Sage.

Aluja-Fabregat, A. (2000). Personality and curiosity about TV and film violence in adolescents. *Personality and Individual Differences, 29,* 379-392.

Aristotle. (1966). De Poetica (I. Bywater, Trans.). In *The works of Aristotle* (vol. 11, chapter 2). Oxford, England: Clarendon.

Arts, W., Hermkens, P., & van Wijck, P. (1995). Anomie, distributive justice and dissatisfaction with material well-being in Eastern Europe. *International Journal of Comparative Sociology, 34,* 1-16.

Ashe, D. D., & McCutcheon, L. E. (2001). Shyness, loneliness, and attitude toward celebrities. *Current Research in Social Psychology, 6,* 124-133.

Austin, B. A. (1985). Loneliness and use of six media among college students. *Psychological Reports, 56,* 323-327.

Auter, P. J., & Davis, D. M. (1991). When characters speak directly to the viewers: Breaking the fourth wall in television. *Journalism Quarterly, 68,* 165-171.

Auter, P. J., & Palmgreen, P. (2000). Development and validation of a parasocial interaction measure: The audience-persona interaction scale. *Communication Research Reports, 17,* 79-89.

Babrow, A. S. (1987). Student motives for watching soap operas. *Journal of Broadcasting and Electronic Media, 31,* 309-321.

Bardo, M. & Mueller, C. (1991). Sensation seeking and drug abuse prevention from a biological perspective. In L. Donohew, H. E. Sypher & W. J. Bukoski (Eds.), *Persuasive communication and drug abuse prevention* (pp. 195-207). Hillsdale, NJ: Erlbaum.

Basil, M. D. (1996). Identification as a mediator of celebrity effects. *Journal of Broadcasting and Electronic Media, 40,* 21-30.

Basil, M. D., & Brown, W. J. (2004). Magic Johnson and Mark McGuire: The power of identification with sports celebrities. In R. Kahle & C. Riley (Eds.), *Sports marketing communication* (pp. 159-171). Mahwah, NJ: Lawrence Erlbaum Associates.

Bell, R. A. (1985). Conversational involvement and loneliness. *Communication Monographs, 52,* 218-235.

Bell, R. A., & Daly, J. A. (1985). Some communicator correlates of loneliness. *Southern Speech Communication Journal, 50,* 121-142.

Bente, G. & Vorderer, P. (1997). The socio-emotional dimension of using screen media. Current perspectives in German media psychology. In P. Winterhoff-Spurk & T. H. A. van der Voort (Eds.), *New horizons in media psychology: Research cooperation and projects in Europe* (pp. 125-144). Opladen, Germany: Westdeutscher Verlag.

Berger, C., & Calabrese, R. (1975). Some explorations in initial interaction and beyond: Toward a developmental theory of interpersonal communication. *Human Communication Research, 1,* 99-112.

Biklen, S. K., & Casella, R. (2007). *A practical guide to the qualitative dissertation.* New York: Teachers College Press.

Biswas, R., Riffe, D., & Zillman, D. (1994). Mood influence on the appeal of bad news. *Journalism Quarterly, 71*(3), 689-696.

Bloom, J. (1996). The O. J. media circus. In J. Gorham (Ed.), *Mass media* (pp. 79-82). New Haven, CT: Dushkin Publishing Group.

Blumler, J. G. (1979). The role of theory in uses and gratifications studies. *Communication Research, 6,* 9-36.

Blumler, J. G. (1985). The social character of media gratifications. In K. E. Rosengren, L. A. Wenner & P. Palmgreen (Eds.), *Media gratifications research: Current Perspectives* (pp. 41-60). Beverly Hills, CA: Sage.

Bogart, L. (1980). Television news as entertainment. In P. H. Tannenbaum (Ed.), *The entertainment functions of television* (pp. 209-249). Hillsdale, NJ: Lawrence Erlbaum.

Boon, S. D., & Lomore, C. D. (2001). Admirer-celebrity relationships among young adults: Explaining perceptions of celebrity influences on identity. *Human Communication Research, 27,* 432-465.

Boorstin, D. (1962). *The image.* New York: Penguin.

Bosshart, L., & Macconi, I. (1998). Defining "Entertainment." *Communication Research Trends, 18*(3), 3-6.

Bowlby, J. (1969). *Attachment and loss: Vol. 1. Attachment* (2nd ed.). New York: Basic Books.

Bowlby, J. (1973). *Attachment and loss: Vol. 2. Separation: Anxiety and anger.* New York: Basic Books.

Bowlby, J. (1988). *A secure base: Parent-child attachment and healthy human development.* New York: Basic Books.

Brewer, W. F. (1996a). The nature of narrative suspense and the problem of rereading. In P. Vorderer, H. J. Wulff & M. Friedrichsen (Eds.), *Suspense: Conceptualizations, theoretical analyses, and empirical explorations* (pp. 107-127). Mahwah, NJ: Lawrence Erlbaum Associates.

Brewer, W. F. (1996b). Good and bad story endings and story completeness. In R. J. Kreuz & M. S. MacNealy (Eds.), *Empirical approaches to literature and aesthetics* (pp. 261-274). Westport, CT: Ablex Publishing.

Brown, W. J., Duane, J. J., & Fraser, B. P. (1997). Media coverage and public opinion of the O. J. Simpson trial: Implications for the criminal justice system. *Communication Law & Policy, 2,* 261-287.

Bryant, J., & Raney, A. A. (2002). Sports on the screen. In D. Zillman & P. Vorderer (Eds.), *Media entertainment: The psychology of its appeal* (pp. 153-174). Mahwah, NJ: Lawrence Erlbaum Associates.

Bryant, J., Roskos-Ewoldson, D., & Cantor, J. (Eds.). (2003). *Communication and emotion: Essays in honor of Dolf Zillman.* Mahwah, NJ: Lawrence Erlbaum Associates.

Bryant, J., & Zillman, D. (1983). Sports violence and the media. In J. H. Goldstein (Ed.), *Sports Violence* (pp. 195-211). New York: Springer-Verlag.

Bryant, J., Zillman, D., & Raney, A. A. (1998). Violence and the enjoyment of media sports. In L. A. Wenner (Ed.), *MediaSport* (pp. 252-265). London: Routledge.

Buhr, T. A., Simpson, T. L., & Pryor, B. (1987). Celebrity endorsers' expertise and perceptions of attractiveness, likeability, and familiarity. *Psychological Reports, 60,* 1307-1309.

Burke, K. (1969). *A rhetoric of motives.* Berkeley: University of California Press.

Cacioppo, J. T., & Petty, R. E. (1982). The need for cognition. *Journal of Personality and Social Psychology, 42,* 116-131.

Cameron, G. L. (1993). Spreading activation and involvement: An experimental test of a cognitive model of involvement. *Journalism Quarterly, 70,* 854-867.

Canary, D. J., & Spitzberg, B. H. (1993). Loneliness and media gratifications. *Communication Research, 20*(6), 800-821.

Caplan, L. (1996). The failure (and promise) of legal journalism. In J. Abramson (Ed.), *Postmortem; The O. J. Simpson case: Justice confronts race, domestic violence, lawyers, money, and the media* (pp. 195-198). New York: Basic Books.

Carlsmith, K. M., Darley J. M., & Robinson, P. H. (2002). Why do we punish? Deterrence and just deserts as motives for punishment. *Journal of Personality and Social Psychology, 83*(2), 284-299.

Casper, J. D., Tyler, T. R., & Fisher, B. (1988). Procedural justice in felony cases. *Law and Society, 22,* 483-507.

Caughey, J. (1984). *Imaginary social worlds: A cultural approach.* Lincoln: University of Nebraska Press.

Caughey, J. L. (1985). Mind games: Imaginary social relationships in American Sport. In G. A. (Ed.), *Meaningful play, playful meaning* (pp. 19-33). Champaign, IL: Human Kinetics Publishers.

Caughey, J. L. (1986). Social relations with media figures. In G. Gumpert & R. Cathcart (Eds.), *Inter/Media. Interpersonal communication in a media world.* New York: Oxford University Press.

Cheek, J. M., & Buss, A. H. (1981). Shyness and sociability. *Journal of Personality and Social Psychology, 41,* 330-339.

Cohen, A. R., Stotland, E., & Wolfe, D. M. (1955). An experimental investigation of need for cognition. *Journal of Abnormal and Social Psychology, 51,* 291-294.

Cohen, J. (2001). Defining identification: A theoretical look at the identification of audiences with media characters. *Mass Communication and Society, 4,* 245-264.

Cohen, J. (2003). Parasocial breakups: Measuring individual differences in responses to the dissolution of parasocial relationships. *Mass Communication and Society, 6,* 191-202.

Cohen, J. (2004). Para-social break-up from favorite television characters: The role of attachment and relationship intensity. *Journal of Social and Personal Relationships, 21,* 187-202.

Cohen, J. (2006). Audience identification with media characters. In J. Bryant & P. Vorderer (Eds.), *Psychology of entertainment* (pp. 183-197). Mahwah, NJ: Lawrence Erlbaum Associates.

Cohen J., & Perse, E. (2003). *Different strokes for different folks: An empirical search for different modes of viewer-character relationships*. Paper presented to the Mass Communication Division at the 53rd annual convention of the International Communication Association (ICA), San Diego, CA, May 24, 2003.

Cole, T., & Leets, L. (1999). Attachment styles and intimate television viewing: Insecurely forming relationships in a parasocial way. *Journal of Social and Personal Relationships, 16*, 495-511.

Compesi, R. J. (1980). Gratifications of daytime TV serial viewers. *Journalism Quarterly, 57*, 155-158.

Comstock, G., & Scharrer, E. (1999). *Television: What's on, who's watching, and what it means*. San Diego, CA: Academic Press.

Cone, J. D., & Foster, S. L. (1993). *Dissertations and theses from start to finish: Psychology and related fields*. Washington, DC: American Psychological Association.

Conway, J. C., & Rubin, A. M. (1991). Psychological predictors of television viewing motivation. *Communication Research, 18*, 443-463.

Cowen, T. (2000). The new heroes and role models: Why separating celebrity from merit is good. *Reason, 32,* 30-36.

Darden, C. (with Walter J.). (1996). *In contempt*. New York: Regan Books.

Darley, J. M., Carlsmith, K. M., & Robinson, P. H. (2000). Incapacitation as just deserts as motives for punishment. *Law and Human Behavior, 24*, 659-684.

Darley, J. M., & Pittman, T. S. (2003). The psychology of compensatory and retributive justice. *Personality and Social Psychology Review, 7*(4), 324-336.

Darlington, R. B. (2006). *Factor analysis*. Retrieved September 22, 2008, from http://www.psych.cornell.edu/Darlington/factor.htm

Denzin, N. K. (1978). *The research act*. New York: McGraw-Hill.

Denzin, N. K. (1989). *Interpretive interactionism*. Applied social research methods series (Vol. 16). Newbury Park, CA: Sage.

Deutsch, M. (1985). *Distributive justice: A social psychological perspective*. New Haven, CT: Yale University Press.

Dominick, J. (1996). *The dynamics of mass communication* (5th ed.). New York: McGraw-Hill.

Donohew, L., Palmgreen, P., & Rayburn, J. D. (1987). Social and psychological origins of media use: A lifestyle analysis. *Journal of Broadcasting and Electronic Media, 31*, 255-278.

Durkheim, E. (1933). *Division of labor in society*. (G. Simpson, Trans.). New York: Free Press. (Original work published in 1893)

Durkheim, E. (1951). *Suicide*. (J. A. Spaulding & G. Simpson, Trans.). New York: Free Press. (Original work published in 1897)

Dyer, R. (1998). *Stars*. London: BFI Publishing.

.Elster, J. (1990). Norms of revenge. *Ethics, 100*, 862-885.

Elster, J. (1992). *Local justice: How institutions allocate scarce goods and necessary burdens*. New York: Russell Sage.

Entman, R. M. (1993). Framing: Towards clarification of a fractures paradigm. *Journal of Communication, 43*(4), 51-58.

104

Epstein, E. J. (2000). *News from nowhere: Television and the news*. Chicago: Ivan R. Dee.

Evans, A., & Wilson, G. D. (1999). *Fame: The psychology of stardom*. London: Vision.

Evans, C. (1981). Justice as deserts. In R. L. Braham (Ed.), *Social justice* (pp. 45-54). Boston: Martinus Nijhoff.

Eyal, K., & Rubin, A. M. (2003). Viewer aggression and homophily, identification, and parasocial relationships with television characters. *Journal of Broadcasting and Electronic Media, 47*(1), 77-98.

Ferle, C. L., Edwards, S. M., & Lee, W. (2000). Teens' use of traditional media and the Internet. *Journal of Advertising Research, 40*(3), 55-65.

Festinger, L. (1957). *A theory of cognitive dissonance*. Stanford, CA: Stanford University Press.

Finn, S., & Gorr, M. B. (1988). Social isolation and social support as correlates of television viewing motives. *Communication Research, 15*, 135-158.

Fischoff, S. F. (1996). Influence of victim reminders on public perception of guilt or non-guilt in a celebrity murder trial. *Journal of Media Psychology, 2*(2), 4-12.

Fishman, M. (1980). *Manufacturing the news*. Austin: University of Texas Press.

Foltin, H. F. (1994). The talkshow in the USA. *Media Perspectives, 8*, 477-487.

Fowles, J. (1992). *Why viewers watch: A reappraisal of television's effects*. Newbury Park, CA: Sage.

Fraser, B. P., & Brown, W. J. (2002). Media celebrities, and social influence: Identification with Elvis Presley. *Mass Communication and Society, 5*(2), 183-206.

French, P. (2001). *The virtues of vengeance*. Lawrence: University of Kansas Press.

Freud, S. (1922/1955). Beyond the pleasure principle. In. J. Strachey (Ed.), *Collected works of Sigmund Freud, Volume 18*. London: Hogarth Press.

Frey, J. H. (1983). *Survey research by telephone*. Beverly Hills, CA: Sage.

Friedman, H., & Friedman, L. (1979). Endorser effectiveness by product type. *Journal of Advertising Research, 19*, 63-71.

Furno-Lamude, D. (1999). The media spectacle and the O. J. Simpson case. In J. Schuete & L. S. Lilley (Eds.), *The O. J. Simpson trials: Rhetoric, media, and the law* (pp. 19-35). Carbondale: Southern Illinois University Press.

Gantz, W. (1981). An exploration of viewing motives and behaviors associated with television sports. *Journal of Broadcasting, 25*, 263-275.

George, D., & Mallery, P. (2008). *SPSS for Windows: Step by step* (8th ed.). Boston: Pearson Education, Inc.

Gerrig, R. J. (1993). *Experiencing narrative worlds*. New Haven, CT: Yale University Press.

Gibbons, J. A., Vogl, R. J., & Grimes, T. (2003). Memory misattributions for characters in a television news story. *Journal of Broadcasting and Electronic Media, 47*(1), 99-112.

Giles, D. (2000). *Illusions of immortality: A psychology of fame and celebrity*. London: MacMillan Press.

Giles, D. C. (2002). Parasocial interaction: A review of the literature and a model for future research. *Media Psychology, 4*, 279-305.

Giles, D. C., & Maltby, J. (2004). The role of media figures in adolescent development: Relations between autonomy, attachment, and interest in celebrities. *Personality and Individual Differences, 36*, 813-822.

Gitlin, T. (1980). *The whole world is watching: Mass media in the making and unmaking of the new left.* Berkeley: University of California Press.

Glatthorn, A. A. (1998). *Writing the winning dissertation: A step-by-step guide.* Thousand Oaks, CA: Corwin Press.

Gleich, V. (1997). *Parasocial interactions and relationships of television viewers.* Landau: Verlag Press.

Goswick, R. A., & Jones, W. H. (1981). Loneliness, self-concept, and adjustment. *Journal of Psychology, 107*, 237-240.

Grace, N. (with Clehane, J.). (2005). *Objection: How high-priced defense attorney's, celebrity defendants, and a 24/7 media have hijacked our criminal justice system.* New York: Hyperion.

Green, M. C., & Brock, T. C. (2000). The role of transportation in the persuasiveness of public narratives. *Journal of Personality and Social Psychology, 79*, 701-721.

Greenberg, B. S., Abelman, R., & Neuendorf, K. (1981). Sex on the soap operas: Afternoon delight. *Journal of Communication, 31*(3), 83-89.

Greenberg, B. S., & D'Alessio, D. (1985). The quantity and quality of sex in the soaps. *Journal of Broadcasting and Electronic Media, 29*, 309-321.

Greenberg, B. S., Neuendorf, K., Buerkel-Rothfuss, N., & Henderson, L. (1982). The soaps: What's on and who cares? *Journal of Broadcasting, 26*, 519-535.

Greenberg, B., & Woods, M. (1999). The soaps: Their sex, gratifications, and outcomes. *Journal of Sex Research, 36*(3), 250-257.

Greenwald, A. G., & Leavitt, C. (1985). Cognitive theory and audience involvement. In L. F. Alwitt & A. A. Mitchell (Eds.), *Psychological processes and advertising effects. Theory, research, and applications* (pp. 221-240). Hillsdale, NJ: Lawrence Erlbaum.

Gross, M. J. (2005). *Starstruck: When a fan gets close to fame.* New York: Bloomsbury.

Guttman, A. (1986). *Sports spectators.* New York: Columbia University Press.

Hair, J. F., Anderson, R. E., Tatham, R. L., & Black, W. C. (1995). *Multivariate data analysis* (4th ed.). Englewood Cliffs, NJ: Prentice Hall.

Henning, B., & Vorderer, P. (2001). Psychological escapism: Predicting the amount of television viewing by need of cognition. *Journal of Communication, 51*, 100-120.

Hoffman, M. L. (1987). The contribution of empathy to justice and moral judgment. In N. Eisenberg & J. Strayer (Eds.), *Empathy and its development* (pp. 47-80). Cambridge, UK: Cambridge University Press.

Hoffner, C. (1996). Children's wishful identifications and parasocial interaction with favorite television characters. *Journal of Broadcasting and Electronic Media, 40*, 389-402.

Hoffner, C., & Cantor, J. (1991). Perceiving and responding to mass media characters. In J. Bryant & D. Zillman (Eds.), *Responding to the screen: Reception and reaction processes* (pp. 63-103). Hillsdale, NJ: Lawrence Erlbaum.

Horowitz, L. M., & French, R. (1979). Interpersonal problems of people who describe themselves as lonely. *Journal of Consulting and Clinical Psychology, 47*, 762-764.

Horton, D., & Wohl, R. (1956). Mass communication and parasocial interaction: Observations on intimacy at a distance. *Psychiatry, 19,* 215-229.

Hurley, D. (1988). The end of celebrity. *Psychology Today, 22,* 50-55.

Huseman, R. C., Hatfield, J. D., & Miles, E. W. (1985). Test for individual perceptions of job equity: Some preliminary findings. *Perceptual and Motor Skills, 61,* 1055-1064.

Huston, A. C., Wright, J. C., Marquis, J., & Green, S. B. (1999). How young children spend their time: Television and other activities. *Developmental Psychology, 35*(4), 912-925.

James, C. (1993). *Fame in the 20th century.* London: BBC Books.

Jones, W. H., Freemon, J. E., & Goswick, R. A. (1981). The persistence of loneliness: Self and other determinants. *Journal of Personality, 49,* 27-48.

Jones, W. H., & Russell, D. (1982). The social reticence scale: An objective measure of shyness. *Journal of Personality Assessment, 46,* 629-631.

Jones, W. H., Rose, J., & Russell, D. (1990). Loneliness and social anxiety. In H. Leitenberg (Ed.), *Handbook of social and evaluation anxiety* (pp. 247-270). New York: Plenum.

Jose, P. E., & Brewer, W. F. (1984). Development of story liking: Character identification, suspense, and outcome resolution. *Developmental Psychology, 20*(5), 911-924.

Kahle, L. R., & Homer, P. M. (1985). Physical attractiveness of the celebrity endorser: A social adaption perspective. *Journal of Consumer Research, 11,* 954-961.

Kahneman, D. Schkade, D., & Sunstein, C. R. (1998). Shared outrage and erratic awards: The psychology of punitive damages. *Journal of Risk and Uncertainty, 16,* 49-86.

Kamins, M. A. (1990). An investigation into the "matchup" hypothesis in celebrity advertising: When beauty may be only skin deep. *Journal of Advertising, 19,* 4-13.

Kamins, M. A., Brand, M. J., Hoeke, S. A., & Moe, J. C. (1989). Two-sided versus one-sided celebrity endorsements: The impact on advertising effectiveness and credibility. *Journal of Advertising, 18,* 4-10.

Kanazawa, S. (2002). Bowling with our imaginary friends. *Evolution and Human Behavior, 23,* 167-171.

Kant, I. (1952). The science of right (W. Hastie, Trans.). In R. Hutchins (Ed.), Great books of the Western world: Vol. 42. *Kant* (pp. 397-446). Chicago: Encyclopedia Brittanica.

Katz, E. (1968). On reopening the question of selectivity in exposure to mass communication. In R. P. Abelson, E. Aronson, W. J. McGuire, T. M. Newcomb, M. J. Rosenberg & P. H. Tannenbaum (Eds.), *Theories of cognitive consistency: A sourcebook* (pp. 788-796). Chicago: Rand McNally.

Katz, E., Blumer, J. G., & Gurevitch, M. (1974). Uses of mass communication by the individual. In W. P. Davison & F. T. C. Yu (Eds.), *Mass communication research: Mass issues and future directions* (pp. 11-35). New York: Praeger.

Katz, E., & Foulkes, D. (1962). On the use of the mass media as "escape": Clarification of a concept. *Public Opinion Quarterly, 26,* 377-388.

Katz, E., Gurevitch, M., & Haas, H. (1973). On the use of mass media for important things. *American Sociological Review, 38,* 164-181.

Kerlinger, F. N. (1979). *Behavioral research: A conceptual approach.* New York : Holt, Rinehart, and Winston.

Kim, Y., & Ross, S. D. (2006). An exploration of motives in sport video gaming. *International Journal of Sports Marketing & Sponsorship, 8,* 34-51.

Kim, Y., Kim, E. Y., & Kang, J. (2003). Teen's mall shopping motivations: Functions of loneliness and media usage. *Family and Consumer Sciences Research Journal, 32,* 140-167.

Kirkpatrick, L. A. (1994). The role of attachment in religious belief and behavior. In K. Bartholomew & D. Perlman (Eds.), Advances in personal relationships: Vol. 5. *Attachment processes in adulthood* (pp. 239-268). London: Kingsley.

Klapper, J. T. (1963). Mass communication research: An old road resurveyed. *Public Opinion Quarterly, 27,* 515-527.

Klimmt, C. (2003). Dimensions and the determinants of the enjoyment of playing digital games: A three-level model. In M. Copier & J. Raessens (Eds.), *Level up: Digital games research conference* (pp. 246-257). Utrecht, Netherlands: Faculty of Arts, Utrecht University.

Klimmt, C., Hartmann, T., & Scrhamm, H. (2006). Parasocial interactions and relationships. In J. Bryant & P. Vorderer (Eds.), *Psychology of entertainment* (pp. 291-313). Mahwah, NJ: Lawrence Erlbaum Associates.

Knolbloch-Westerwick, S. (2006). Mood management theory, evidence, and advancements. In J. Bryant & P. Vorderer (Eds.), *Psychology of entertainment* (pp. 239-254). Mahwah, NJ: Lawrence Erlbaum.

Kubey, R. W. (1986). Television use in everyday life: Coping with unstructured time. *Journal of Communication, 36*(3), 108-121.

Kurdek, L. (1987). Gender differences in the psychological symptomatology and coping strategies of young adolescents. *Journal of Early Adolescents, 7,* 395-410.

LaFave, W. (2000). *Criminal law* (3rd ed.). St. Paul, MN: West.

Lee, K. M. (2004). Presence explicated. *Communication Theory, 14*(1), 27-50.

Leigh-Kile, D. (1999). *Sex Symbols.* London: Vision Paperbacks.

Lerner, M. J. (1977). The justice motive: Some hypotheses as to its origins and forms. *Journal of Personality, 45,* 1-51.

Lerner, M. J. (1980). *The belief in a just world: A fundamental delusion.* New York: Plenum.

Lerner, M. J. (2003). The justice motive: Where social psychologists found it, how they lost it, and why they may not find it again. *Personality and Social Psychology Review, 7*(4), 388-399.

Leventhal, G. S. (1976). Fairness in social relationships. In J. W. Thibaut, J. T. Spence & R. C. Carson (Eds.), *In contemporary topics in social psychology* (pp. 212-239). Morristown, NJ: General Learning.

Leventhal, G. S. (1980). What should be done with equity theory? New approaches to the study of fairness in social relationships. In K. J. Gergen, M. S. Greenberg & R. H. Willis (Eds.), *Social exchange* (pp. 27-55). New York: Plenum.

Levy, M. R. (1979). Watching TV news as para-social interaction. *Journal of Broadcasting, 27,* 68-80.

Lewis, M., Dyer, C. L., & Moran, J. D. (1995). Parental and peer influences on the clothing purchases of female adolescent consumers as a function of discretionary income. *Journal of Family and Consumer Sciences, 87*, 15-20.

Lind, A. E.., Kurtz, S., Musante, L., Walker, L., & Thibaut, J. W. (1980). Procedure and outcome effects on reactions to adjudicated resolution of conflicts of interest. *Journal of Personality and Social Psychology, 39*(4), 643-653.

Lind, A. E., Maccoun, R. J., Ebener, P. A., Felstiner, W. L. F., Hensler, D. R., Resnik, J., & Tyler, T. R. (1990). In the eye of the beholder: Tort litigants' evaluations of their experiences in the civil justice system. *Law and Society Review, 24*(4), 953-988.

Lind, A. E., & Tyler, T. R. (1988). *The social psychology of procedural justice.* New York: Plenum.

Livingstone, S. M. (1998). Relationships between media and audiences: Prospects for audience reception research. In T. Liebes & J. Curran (Eds.), *Media, ritual, and identity* (pp. 237-255). London: Routledge.

Lo, V. (1994). Media use involvement, and knowledge of the gulf war. *Journalism Quarterly, 71*, 43-54.

Loucks, S. (1980). Loneliness, affect, and self-concept: Construct validity of the Bradley loneliness scale. *Journal of Personality Assessment, 44*, 142-147.

Lowenthal, L. (1961). *Literature, popular culture, and society.* Englewood Cliffs, NJ: Prentice-Hall.

Lull, J. (1980). The social uses of television. *Human Communication Research, 6*, 197-209.

Maes, J. (1994). Blaming the victim – belief in control or belief in justice? *Social Justice Research, 7*, 69-90.

Major, B., & Deaux, K. (1982). Individual differences in justice behavior. In J. Greenberg & R. L. Cohen (Eds.), *Equity and justice in social behavior* (pp. 43-76). New York: Academic Press.

Maltby, J., Houran, J., Lange, R., Ashe, D., & McCutcheon, L. E. (2002). Thou shalt worship no other gods – unless they are celebrities: The relationship between celebrity worship and religious orientation. *Personality and Individual Differences, 32*, 1157-1172.

Maslow, A. H. (1943). A theory of human motivation. *Psychological Review, 50*(4), 370-396.

McCain, T. A., Chilberg, J., & Wakshlag, J. (1977). The effect of camera angle on source credibility and attraction. *Journal of Broadcasting, 21*, 35-46.

McCombs, M. (2004). *Setting the agenda: The mass media and public opinion.* Malden, MA: Polity.

McCourt, A., & Fitzpatrick, J. (2001). The role of personal characteristics and romantic characteristics in parasocial relationships: A pilot. *Journal of Mundane Behavior*, Article 2.1. Retrieved May 30, 2007, from http://mundanebehavior.org/issues/v2nl/mccourt_fitzpatrick.html

McCutcheon, L. E., Ashe, D. D., Houran., & Maltby, J. (2003). A cognitive profile of individuals who tend to worship celebrities. *The Journal of Psychology, 137*(4), 309-322.

McCutcheon, L. E., Lange, R., & Houran, J. (2002). Conceptualization and measurement of celebrity worship. *British Journal of Psychology*, 93, 67-87.

McDaniel, S. R. (2003). Reconsidering the relationship between sensation seeking and audience preferences for viewing televised sports. *Journal of Sport Management*, *17*, 13-36.

Mcfarlin, D. B., & Sweeney, P. D. (1992). Distributive and procedural justice as predictors of satisfaction with personal and organizational outcomes. *Academy of Management Journal*, *35*, 626-637.

Mcguire, W. (1974). Psychological motives and communication gratification. In J. Blumler & E. Katz (Eds.), *The uses of mass communication: Current perspectives* (pp. 167-195). Beverly Hills, CA: Sage.

McIlwraith, R. D. (1998). "I'm addicted to television": The personality, imagination, and TV watching patterns of self-identified TV addicts. *Journal of Broadcasting*, *42*, 371-386.

McLeod, J. M., & Becker, L. B. (1974). Testing the validity of gratifications measures through political effects analysis. In J. G. Blumler & E. Katz (Eds.), *The uses of mass communications: Current perspectives on gratifications research*. Beverly Hills, CA: Sage.

McQuail, D. (1994). *Mass communication theory: An introduction* (3rd ed.). Thousand Oaks, CA: Sage.

McQuail, D., Blumler, J. G., & Brown, J. R. (1972). The television audience: A revised perspective. In D. McQuail (Ed.), *Sociology of mass communications* (pp. 121-153). Middlesex, England: Penguin.

McWhirter, B. T. (1997). Loneliness, learned resourcefulness, and self-esteem in college students. *Journal of Counseling & Development*, *75*(6), 460-469.

Mendelsohn, H. A. (1964). Listening to radio. In A. Lewis Dexter & D. White (Eds.). *People, society, and mass communication* (pp. 89-98). London: Collier-Macmillan.

Metzger, M. J. (2002). When no news is good news: Inferring closure for news issues. *Journalism & Mass Communication Quarterly*, *77*(4), 760-787.

Merriam-Webster's Collegiate Dictionary (11th ed.). (2003). Springfield, MA: Merriam-Webster.

Mikula, G., Scherer, K. R., & Athenstaedt, V. (1998). The role of injustice in the elicitation of differential emotional reactions. *Personality and Social Psychology Bulletin*, *24*, 769-783.

Mikulincer, M., & Segal, J. (1990). A multidimensional analysis of the experience of loneliness. *Journal of Social and Personal Relationships*, 7, 209-230.

Mill, J. S. (1957). *Utilitarianism*. New York: Bobbs-Merrill.

Miller, D. T. (2001). Disrespect and the experience of injustice. *Annual Review of Psychology*, *52*, 527-553.

Miller, W. I. (1998). Clint Eastwood and equity: Popular culture's theory of revenge. In A. Sarat & T. R. Kearns (Eds.). *Law in the domains of culture* (pp. 161-202). Ann Arbor: The University of Michigan Press.

Misra, S. (1990). Celebrity spokesperson and brand congruence: An assessment of recall and affect. *Journal of Business Research*, 21, 159-173.

Mitroff, D. & Bennis, W. (1989). *The unreality industry: The deliberate manufacturing of falsehood and what it is doing to our lives.* New York: Birch Lane Press.

Montaigne, M. (1958). *The complete works of Montaigne: Essays, travel, journal, letters* (D. M. Frame, Trans.). Stanford, CA: Stanford University Press.

Morgan, M. (1984). Heavy television viewing and perceived quality of life. *Journalism Quarterly, 61,* 499-504.

Morton, J. (1997). Don't worry, it will go away. American Journalism Review, *19,* 52.

Moulton, D., & O'Connor, C. (2006). *Celebrity court cases: Trials of the rich and famous.* Alberta, Canada: Altitude Publishing.

Nagin, D. (1998). Deterrence and incapacitation. In M. Tonry (Ed.), *The handbook of crime and punishment* (pp. 345-368). New York: Oxford University Press.

Neuman, R. W., Just, M. R., & Crigler, A. N. (1992). *Common knowledge. News and the construction of political meaning.* Chicago: University of Chicago Press.

Nielson, A. C. (1994). *Reference supplement: Nielsen station index.* New York: Nielsen Media Research.

Nordlund, J. (1978). Media interaction. *Communication Research,* 5, 150-175.

Oetting, E., & Donnermeyer, J. F. (1998). Primary socialization theory: The etiology of drug use and deviance, vol. 1. *Substance Use and Misuse, 33,* 995-1026.

Oliver, M. B. (1996). Influences of authoritarianism and portrayals of race on Caucasian viewers' responses to reality-based crime dramas. *Communication Reports, 9*(2), 141-150.

Oliver, M. B., Kim, J., & Sanders, M. S. (2006). Personality. In J. Bryant & P. Vorderer (Eds.), *Psychology of entertainment* (pp. 329-341). Mahwah, NJ: Lawrence Erlbaum.

Olson, B. (1994). Soaps, sex, and cultivation. *Mass Communication Review, 21,* 106-113.

Osawld, M. E., Hupfeld, J., Klug, S. C., & Gabriel, U. (2002). Lay perspective on criminal deviance, goals of punishment, and punitivity. *Social Justice Research, 15,* 85-98.

Palmgreen, P., & Rayburn, J. D. (1979). Uses and gratifications and exposure to public television. *Communication Research, 6,* 155-179.

Palmgreen, P., Wenner, L. A., & Rayburn, J. D. (1980). Relations between gratifications sought and obtained: A study of television news. *Communication Research, 7*(2), 161-192.

Park, C. W., & McClung, G. W. (1986). The effect of TV program involvement on involvement with commercials. *Advances in Consumer Research, 13,* 544-548.

Peplau, L. A., Russell, D., & Heim, M. (1978). Loneliness: A bibliography of research and theory. JSAS. *Catalog of Selected Documents in Psychology, 8,* 38.

Peplau, L. A., Russell, D., & Heim, M. (1979). The experience of loneliness. In I. H. Frieze, D. Bar-tal & J. S. Carroll (Eds.), *New approaches to social problems* (pp. 53-78). San Francisco, CA: Jossey-Bass.

Perlman, D., & Peplau, L. A. (1981). Toward a social psychology of loneliness. In R. Gilmour & S. Duck (Eds.), *Personal relationships, 3: Personal relationships in disorder* (pp. 31-56). London: Academic Press.

Perloff, R. M., Quarles, R. C., & Drutz, M. (1983). Loneliness, depression, and the uses of television. *Journalism Quarterly, 60,* 352-356.

Perse, E. M. (1990a). Audience selectivity and involvement in the newer media environment. *Communication Research, 17*, 675-697.

Perse, E. M. (1990b). Cultivation and involvement with local television news. In N. Signorielli & M. Morgan (Eds.), *Advances in cultivation analysis* (pp. 51-69). Newbury Park, CA: Sage.

Perse, E. M. (1990c). Involvement with local television news: Cognitive and emotional dimensions. *Human Communication Research, 16*(4). 556-581.

Perse, E. M. (1990d). Media involvement and local television news effects. *Journal of Broadcasting and Electronic Media, 34*, 17-36.

Perse, E. M., & Rubin, A. M. (1988). Audience activity and satisfaction with favorite television soap operas. *Journalism Quarterly, 65*, 368-375.

Perse, E. M., & Rubin, R. B. (1989). Attribution in social and parasocial relationships. *Communication Research, 16*, 59-77.

Perse, E. M., & Rubin, A. M. (1990). Chronic loneliness and television use. *Journal of Broadcasting and Electronic Media, 34*, 37-53.

Pervin, L. A., & John, O. P. (2001). *Personality: Theory and research.* New York: John Wiley & Sons, Inc.

Petty, R. E., Ostrom, T. M., & Brock, T. C. (Eds.). (1981). *Cognitive responses in persuasion.* Hillsdale, NJ: Sage.

Postman, N. (1985). *Amusing ourselves to death.* New York: Penguin.

Potter, W. J. (2004). *Theory of media literacy: A cognitive approach.* Thousand Oaks, CA: Sage.

Powers, R. (1978). *The newscasters: The news business as show business.* New York: St. Martin's Press.

Rader, B. G. (1984). *In its own image: How television has transformed sports.* New York: Free Press.

Raney, A. A. (2002). Moral judgment as a predictor of enjoyment of crime drama. *Media Psychology, 4*, 305-322.

Raney, A. A. (2003). Disposition-based theories of enjoyment. In J. Bryant, D. Roskos-Ewoldsen, & J. R. Cantor (Eds.), *Communication and emotion: Essays in honor of Dolf Zillman* (pp. 397-416). Mahwah, NJ: Lawrence Erlbaum.

Raney, A. A. (2004). Expanding disposition theory: Reconsidering character liking, moral evaluations, and enjoyment. *Communication Theory, 14*, 348-369.

Raney, A. A. (2005). Punishing media criminals and moral judgment: The impact on enjoyment. *Media Psychology, 7*(2), 145-163.

Raney, A. A. (2006). The psychology of disposition-based theories of media enjoyment. In J. Bryant & P. Vorderer (Eds.), *Psychology of entertainment* (pp. 137-150). Mahwah, NJ: Lawrence Erlbaum Associates.

Raney, A. A., & Bryant, J. (2002). Moral judgment and crime drama: An integrated theory of enjoyment. *Journal of Communication, 52*, 402-415.

Rantala, M. L. (1996). *O. J. unmasked: The trial, the truth, and the media.* Chicago: Catfeet Press.

Ray, M. L. (1973). Marketing communication and the hierarchy-of-effects. In P. Clarke (Ed.), *New models for communication research* (pp. 147-176). Beverly Hills, CA: Sage.

Reeve, J. (1996). *Motivating others*. Needham Heights, MA: Allyn & Bacon.

Reeves, B., & Nass, C. (1996). *The media equation: How people treat computers, television, and new media like real people and places*. New York: Cambridge University Press.

Rhodes, N., & Hamilton, J. C. (2006). Attribution and entertainment: It's not who dunnit, it's why. In J. Bryant & P. Vorderer (Eds.), *Psychology of entertainment* (pp. 119-136). Mahwah, NJ: Lawrence Erlbaum.

Richins, M. L., Bloch, P. H., & McQuarrie, E. F. (1992). How enduring and situational involvement combine to create involvement responses. *Journal of Consumer Psychology, 1*, 143-153.

Robinson, J. D., & Skill, T. (1995). Media usage patterns and portrayals of the elderly. In *Handbook of communication and aging research*. Mahwah, NJ: Lawrence Erlbaum Associates.

Robinson, J. P., & Davis, D. K. (1990). Television news and the informed public: An information processing approach. *Journal of Communication, 40*(3), 106-119.

Robinson, P. H., & Darley, J. M. (1995). *Justice, liability, and blame: Community views and the criminal law*. Boulder, CO: Westview.

Robinson, P. H., & Darley, J. M. (1997). The utility of desert. *Northwestern University Law Review, 91*, 453-499.

Rojek, C. (2006). Sports celebrity and the civilizing process. *Sport and Society, 9*(4), 674-690.

Rook, K. S., & Peplau, L. A. (1982). Perspectives on helping the lonely. In L. A. Peplau & D. Perlman (Eds.), Loneliness: A sourcebook of current theory, research, and therapy (pp. 351-378). New York: Wiley.

Rosengren, K. E. (1974). Uses and gratifications: A paradigm outlined. In J. Blumler & E. Katz (Eds.), *The uses of mass communication: Current perspectives* (pp. 269-286). Beverly Hills, CA: Sage.

Rosengren, K. E., & Wenner, L. E., & Palmgreen, P. (1985). *Media gratifications research: Current perspectives*. Beverly Hills, CA: Sage.

Rosengren, K. E., & Windahl, S. (1972). Mass media consumption as a functional alternative. In D. McQuail (Ed.), *Sociology of mass communications* (pp. 166-194). Middlesex, England: Penguin.

Roser, C. (1990). Involvement, attention, and perception of message relevance in the response to persuasive appeals. *Communication Research, 17*, 571-600.

Rossi, P. H., Berk, R. E., & Campbell, A. (1997). Just punishments: Guideline sentences and normative consensus. *Journal of Quantitative Criminology, 13*, 267-290.

Rothenbuhler, E. W. (1985). Media events and social solidarity: An updated report on the living room celebration of the Olympic Games. Paper presented at the annual meeting of the International Communication Association, Chicago.

Rubin, A. M. (1976). A developmental examination of the use of television by children and adolescents. Unpublished doctoral dissertation, University of Illinois.

Rubin, A. M. (1979). Television use by children and adolescents. *Human Communication Research, 5*, 109-120.

Rubin, A. M. (1981). An examination of television viewing motivations. *Communication Research, 8*, 141-165.

Rubin, A. M. (1983). Television uses and gratifications: The interactions of viewing patterns and motivations. *Journal of Broadcasting, 24*, 37-51.

Rubin, A. M. (1984). Ritualized and instrumental television viewing. *Journal of Communication, 34*, 67-77.

Rubin, A. M. (1985). Uses of television daytime soap operas by college students. *Journal of Broadcasting and Electronic Media, 29*, 241-258.

Rubin, A. M. (2002). The uses-and-gratifications perspective of media effects. In J. Bryant & D. Zillman (Eds.), *Media effects: Advances in theory and research* (pp. 525-548). Mahwah, NJ: Lawrence Erlbaum Associates.

Rubin, A. M., Haridakis, P. M., & Eyal, K. (2003). Viewer aggression and attraction to television talk shows. *Media Psychology, 5*, 331-362.

Rubin, A. M., & Perse, E. M. (1987). Audience activity and television news gratifications. *Communication Research, 14*, 58-84.

Rubin, A. M., Perse, E. M., & Powell, R. A. (1985). Loneliness, parasocial interaction, and local television news viewing. *Human Communication Research, 12*, 155-180.

Rubin, A. M., & Rubin, R. B. (1982). Contextual age and television use. *Human Communication Research, 8*, 228-244.

Rubin, A. M., & Rubin, R. B. (1985). Interface of personal and mediated communication: A research agenda. Critical Studies in Mass Communication, *2*, 36-53.

Rubin, R. B., & McHugh, M. P. (1987). Development of parasocial interaction relationships. *Journal of Broadcasting and Electronic Media, 31*, 279-292.

Rubin, R. B., & Rubin, A. M. (1982). Contextual age and television use: Reexamining a life-position indicator. In M. Burgoon (Ed.), *Communication yearbook 6* (pp. 583-604). Beverly Hills, CA: Sage.

Rubin, R. B., & Rubin, M. (2001). Attribution in social and parasocial relationships. In V. Manusou & J. H. Harvey (Eds.), *Attribution, communication behavior, and close relationships* (pp. 320-337). Cambridge, UK: Cambridge University Press.

Rubin, Z. (1979). Seeking a cure for loneliness. *Psychology Today, 13*, 82-90.

Rubin, Z., & Peplau, L. A. (1973). Belief in a just world and reactions to another's lot: A study of participants in the National Draft Lottery. *Journal of Social Issues, 29*(4), 73-93.

Rubinstein, C., & Shaver, P. (1982). *In search of intimacy.* New York: Delacorte.

Rummel, R. J. (1984). *Applied factor analysis.* Evanston, IL: Northwestern University Press.

Russell, D., Peplau, L. A., & Cutrona, C. E. (1980). The Revised UCLA Loneliness Scale: Concurrent and discriminant validity evidence. *Journal of Personality and Social Psychology, 39*, 472-480.

Ryan, R. M. (1982). Control and information in the intrapersonal sphere: An extension of cognitive evaluation theory. *Journal of Personality and Social Psychology, 43*, 450-461.

Ryan, R. M., & Deci, E. L. (2000). Self-determination theory and the facilitation of intrinsic motivations, social development, and well-being. *American Psychologist, 1*, 68-78.

114

Salmon, C. T. (1986). Perspectives on involvement in consumer and communication research. In B. Dervin & M. J. Voigt (Eds.), *Progress in communication sciences* (pp. 243-268). Beverly Hills, CA: Sage.

Sapolsky, B. S. (1980). The effect of spectator disposition and suspense on the enjoyment of sports contests. *International Journal of Sport Psychology, 11*(1), 1-10.

Sargent, S. L. Zillman, D., & Weaver, J. B. (1998). The gender gap in the enjoyment of televised sports. *Journal of Sport & Social Issues, 22,* 46-64.

Scheff, T. J. (1979). *Catharsis, in healing, ritual, and drama.* Berkeley: University of California Press.

Scheufele, D. A. (1999). Framing as a theory of media effects. *Journal of Communication, 49,* 102-122.

Schmitt, M. (1996). Individual differences in sensitivity to befallen injustice (SBI). *Personality and Individual Differences, 21,* 3-20.

Schmitt, M., & Dörfel, M. (1999). Procedural injustice at work; justice sensitivity, job satisfaction and psychosomatic well-being. *European Journal of Social Psychology, 29,* 443-453.

Schmitt, M., & Maes, J. (2006). Equity and justice. In J. Bryant & P. Vorderer (Eds.), *Psychology of entertainment* (pp. 273-289). Mahwah, NJ: Lawrence Erlbaum.

Schmitt, M. & Sabbagh, C. (2004). Synergistic x situation interaction in distributive justice judgment and allocation behaviour. *Personality and Individual Differences, 37,* 359-371.

Schuetz, J. (1994). *The logic of women on trial: Case studies of popular American trials.* Carbondale: Southern Illinois University Press.

Schuetz, J. (1999). Introduction: Telelitigation and its challenges to trial discourse. In J. Schuetz & L. S. Lilley (Eds.), *The O. J. Simpson Trials: Rhetoric, media, and the law* (pp. 1-18). Carbondale: Southern Illinois University Press.

Schultz, N. R., & Moore, D. (1984). Loneliness: Correlates, attributions, and coping among older adults. *Personality and Social Psychology Bulletin, 10,* 67-77.

Schultze, Q. J. (1991). *Televangelism and American culture.* Grand Rapids, MI: Baker Books.

Schumacher, H. (1992). Moderation in magazine. In K. Hickethier (Ed.), *Programming and Marketing* (pp. 193-209). Frankfurt, Germany: Lang.

Sermat, V. (1978). Sources of loneliness. *Essence, 2,* 271-276.

Sermat, V. (1980). Some situational and personality correlates of loneliness. In J. Hartog, J. R. Audy & Y. A. Cohen (Eds.), *The anatomy of loneliness* (pp. 305-318). New York: International University Press.

Shah, D. V., Watts, M. D., Domke, D., & Fan, D. P. (2002). News framing and cueing of issue regimes. *Public Opinion Quarterly, 66,* 339-370.

Sharkey, J. (1993, December). When pictures drive foreign policy: Somalia raises serious questions about media influence. *American Journalism Review,* pp. 14-19.

Shaw, D. (1995, October 9). Obsession: Did the media overfeed a starving public? *Los Angeles Times* (special reports), pp. S1-S12.

Shim, J. W., & Paul, B. (2007). Effects of personality types on the use of television genre. *Journal of Broadcasting & Electronic Media, 51*(2), 287-304.

Shivers, J. S. (1979). The origin of man, culture, and leisure. In H. Ibrahim & J. S. Shivers (Eds.), *Leisure: Emergence and expansion* (pp. 3-44). Los Alamitos, CA: Hwong.

Shoemaker, P. J., Schooler, C., & Danielson, W. A. (1989). Involvement with the media. Recall versus recognition of election information. *Communication Research, 16,* 78-103.

Slater, M. D. (2002). Involvement as goal-directed strategic processing. Extending the elaboration likelihood model. In J. P. Dillard & M. Pfau (Eds.), *The persuasion handbook. Developments in theory and practice* (pp. 175-194). Thousand Oaks, CA: Sage.

Snodgrass, M. A. (1989). The relationships of differential loneliness, intimacy, and characterological attributional style to duration of loneliness. In M. Hojat & R. Crandall (Eds.), *Loneliness: Theory, research, and applications* (pp. 173-186). Newbury Park, CA: Sage.

Snow, R. P. (1983). *Creating media culture*. Beverly Hills, CA: Sage.

Sparks, G. G., & Sparks, C. W. (2000). Violence, mayhem, & horror. In D. Zillman & P. Vorderer (Eds.), *Media entertainment: The psychology of its appeal* (pp. 73-91). Mahwah, NJ: Lawrence Erlbaum.

Spitzberg, B. H., & Canary, D. J. (1985). Loneliness and relationally competent communication. *Journal of Social and Personal Relationships, 2,* 387-402.

Spitzberg, B. H., & Hurt, H. T. (1989). The relationship of interpersonal competence and skills to reported loneliness across time. In M. Hojat & R. Crandall (Eds.), *Loneliness: Theory, research, and applications* (pp. 157-172). Newbury Park, CA: Sage.

Stever, G. S. (1991). The celebrity appeal questionnaire. *Psychological Reports, 68,* 859-866.

Sullivan, D. B. (1991). Commentary and viewer perception of player hostility: Adding punch to televised sport. *Journal of Broadcasting and Electronic Media, 35,* 487-504.

Surette, R. (1989). Media trials. *Journal of Criminal Justice, 17,* 293-308.

Swanson, D. L. (1977). The uses and misuses of uses and gratifications. *Human Communication Research, 3,* 214-221.

Television Bureau of Advertising. (2005). *Trends in television.* New York: Author.

The Simpson Legacy. (1995, October 8-11). *Los Angeles Times,* section S.

Thibaut, T., & Walker, L. A. (1975). *Procedural justice: A psychological analysis.* New York: Erlbaum/Halstead.

Thibaut, J., & Walker, L. A. (1978). A theory of procedure. *California Law Review, 66,* 541-566.

Törmblom, K. Y. (1992). The social psychology of distributive justice. In K. Scherer (Ed.), *Justice: Interdisciplinary perspectives* (pp. 175-236). Cambridge, England: Cambridge University Press.

Tsao, J. (1996). Compensatory media use: An exploration of two paradigms. *Communication Studies, 47,* 89-109.

Tudor, A. (1974). *Image and influence: Studies in the sociology of film.* London: Allen & Unwin.

Turner, J. R. (1993). Interpersonal and psychological predictors of parasocial interaction with different television performers. *Communication Quarterly, 41*, 443-453.

Tyler, T. R. (1984). The role of perceived injustice in defendants' evaluations of their courtroom experience. *Law and Society Review, 18*, 53-75.

Tyler, T. R. (1988). What is procedural justice?: Criteria used by citizens to assess the fairness of legal procedures. *Law and Society Review, 22*, 103-137.

Tyler, T. R. (1989). The psychology of procedural justice: A test of the group value model. *Journal of Personality and Social Psychology, 57*, 830-838.

Tyler, T. R. (1994). Psychological models of the justice motive: Antecedents of distributive and procedural justice. *Journal of Personality and Social Psychology, 67*(5), 850-863.

Tyler, T. R., Degoey, P., & Smith, H. (1996). Understanding why the justice of group procedures matters: A test of the psychological dynamics of the group-value model. *Journal of Personality and Social Psychology, 70*, 913-930.

Tyler, T. R., & Smith, H. (1998). Social justice and social movements. In D. T. Gilbert, S. T. Fiske & G. Lindzey (Eds.), *The handbook of social psychology* (Vol. II, pp. 595-629). Oxford, England: Oxford University Press.

Tyler, T. R., & Weber, R. (1983). Support for the death penalty. *Law and Society Review, 17*, 201-224.

Uelman, G. F. (1996). *Lessons from the trial: O. J. Simpson* Kansas City, KS: Andrews and McMeel.

Valkenburg, P. M., & Peter, J. (2006). Fantasy and imagination. In J. Bryant & P. Vorderer (Eds.), *Psychology of Entertainment* (pp. 105-117). Mahwah, NJ: Lawrence Erlbaum.

Vermut, R., & Steensma, H. (Eds.). (1991). *Social justice in human relations: Societal and psychological origins of justice*. New York: Academic Press.

Vidmar, N. (2001). Retribution and revenge. In J. Sanders & V. L. Hamilton (Eds.), *Handbook of justice research in law* (pp. 31-63). New York: Kluwer Academic/ Plenum.

Vidmar, N. (2002). Retributive justice: Its social context. In M. Ross & D. T. Miller (Eds.), *The justice motive in everyday life* (pp. 291-313). New York: Cambridge University Press.

Visscher, A., & Vorderer, P. (1998). Parasocial relations. In H. Willems & M. Jurga (Eds.), *The staged society* (pp. 453-469). Wiesbaden, Germany: Verlag.

Vorderer, P. (1996). *TV as relationship machine: Parasocial relationships and interactions with TV personae*. Opladen, Germany: Verlag.

Vorderer, P., & Groeben, N. (1992). Audience research: What the humanistic and the social science approaches could learn from each other. *Poetics, 21*, 361-376.

Vorderer, P., & Knolbloch, S. (2000). Conflict and suspense in drama. In D. Zillman & P. Vorderer (Eds.), *Media entertainment: The psychology of its appeal* (pp. 59-72). Mahwan, NJ: Lawrence Erlbaum Associates.

Vorderer, P., Steen, F. F., & Chan, E. (2006). Motivation. In J. Bryant & P. Vorderer (Eds.), *Psychology of entertainment* (pp. 3-17). Mahwah, NJ: Lawrence Erlbaum Associates.

Wahl, O. F. (1995). Media madness: Public images of mental illness. New Brunswick, NJ: Rutgers University Press.

Wampold, B. E., Davis, B., & Good, R. H. (1990). Hypothesis validity of clinical research. *Journal of Consulting and Clinical Psychology, 58*, 360-367.

Watkins, B. (1988). Children's representations of television and real-life stories. *Communication Research, 2*, 159-185.

Wenner, L. A., & Gantz, W. (1989). The audience experience with sports on television. In L. A. Wenner (Ed.), *Experience with sports on television* (pp. 241-269). Newbury Park, CA: Sage.

Wicks, R. H. (2006). Media information processing. In J. Bryant & P. Vorderer (Eds.), *Psychology of entertainment* (pp. 85-102). Mahwan, NJ: Lawrence Erlbaum.

Wilson, T. (1993). *Watching television: Hermeneutics, reception, and popular culture.* Cambridge, UK: Polity Press.

Wirth, W. (2006). Involvement. In J. Bryant & P. Vorderer (Eds.), *Psychology of entertainment* (pp. 199-213). Mahwah, NJ: Lawrence Erlbaum Associates.

Woods, M. G. (1998). Teen viewing of soaps: A uses and gratifications/cultivation study. International Communication Association Annual Conference. Jerusalem, Israel.

Zaichkowsky, J. L. (1986). Conceptualizing involvement. *Journal of Advertising, 15*, 14-34.

Zillman, D. (1985). The experimental exploration of gratifications from media entertainment. In K. E. Rosengren, L. A. Wenner, & P. Palmgreen (Eds.), *Media gratifications research: Current perspectives* (pp. 225-239). Beverly Hills, CA: Sage.

Zillman, D. (1988a). Mood management: Using entertainment to full advantage. In L. Donohew, H. E. Sypher & E. T. Higgins (Eds.), *Communication, social cognition, and affect* (pp. 147-171). Hillsdale, NJ: Lawrence Erlbaum.

Zillman, D. (1988b). Mood management through communication choices. *American Behavioral Scientist, 31*(3), 327-340.

Zillman, D. (1991). Empathy: Affect from bearing witness to the emotions of others. In J. Bryant & D. Zillman (Eds.), *Responding to the screen: Reception and reaction processes* (pp. 135-167). Hillsdale, NJ: Erlbaum.

Zillman, D. (1994). Mechanisms of emotional involvement with drama. *Poetics, 23*, 33-51.

Zillman, D. (1996). The psychology of suspense in dramatic exposition. In P. Vorderer, H. J. Wulff & M. Friedrichsen (Eds.), *Suspense: Conceptualizations, theoretical analyses, and empirical explorations* (pp. 199-231). Mahwah, NJ: Lawrence Erlbaum.

Zillman, D. (1998). The psychology of the appeal of portrayals of violence. In J. H. Goldstein (Ed.), *Why we watch: The attraction of violent entertainment* (pp. 179-211). New York: Oxford University Press.

Zillman, D. (2000a). The coming of media entertainment. In D. Zillman & P. Vorderer (Eds.), *Media entertainment: The psychology of its appeal* (pp. 1-20). Mahwah, NJ: Lawrence Erlbaum Associates.

Zillman, D. (2000b). Humor and comedy. In D. Zillman & P. Vorderer (Eds.), *Media entertainment: The psychology of its appeal* (pp. 37-57). Mahwah, NJ: Lawrence Erlbaum.

Zillman, D. (2000c). Basil morality in drama appreciation. In I. Bondebjerg (Ed.), *Moving images, culture, and the mind* (pp. 53-63). Luton, England: University of Luton Press.

Zillman, D. (2000d). Mood management in the context of selective exposure theory. In M. F. Roloff (Ed.), *Communication yearbook 23* (pp. 103-123). Thousand Oaks, CA: Sage.

Zillman, D., Bryant, J., & Sapolsky, B. S. (1979). The enjoyment of watching sports contests. In J. H. Goldstein (Ed.), *Sports, games, and play: Social and psychological viewpoints* (pp. 297-335). Hillsdale, NJ: Lawrence Erlbaum.

Zillman, D., Bryant, J., & Sapolsky, B. S. (1989). Enjoyment from sport spectatorship. In J. H. Goldstein (Ed.), *Sports, games, and play: Social and psychological viewpoints* (2nd ed., pp. 241-278). Hillsdale, NJ: Lawrence Erlbaum Associates.

Zillman, D., Taylor, K., & Lewis, K. (1998). News as nonfiction theater: How dispositions toward the public cast of characters affect reactions. *Journal of Broadcasting and Electronic Media, 42*(2), 153-169.

Zuckerman, M. (1996). Sensation seeking and the taste for vicarious horror. In J. B. Weaver III & R. Tamborini (Eds.), *Horror films: Current research on audience preferences and reactions* (pp. 147-160). Mahwah, NJ: Lawrence Erlbaum.

www.ingramcontent.com/pod-product-compliance
Lightning Source LLC
Chambersburg PA
CBHW020915090426
42736CB00008B/646